Stardust girl

Stardust girl

a memoir

Jan Welles

alyson books

los angeles | new york

MANUFACTURED IN THE UNITED STATES OF AMERICA.

THIS TRADE PAPERBACK ORIGINAL IS PUBLISHED BY ALYSON PUBLICATIONS,
P.O. BOX 4371, LOS ANGELES, CA 90078-4371.
DISTRIBUTION IN THE UNITED KINGDOM BY
TURNAROUND PUBLISHER SERVICES LTD.,
UNIT 3, OLYMPIA TRADING ESTATE, COBURG ROAD, WOOD GREEN,
LONDON N22 6TZ ENGLAND.

FIRST EDITION: NOVEMBER 2001

01 02 03 04 05 a 10 9 8 7 6 5 4 3 2 1

ISBN 1-55583-627-5

LIBRARY OF CONGRESS CATALOGING-IN-PUBLICATION DATA
WELLES, JAN.
  STARDUST GIRL : A MEMOIR / BY JAN WELLES.—1ST ED.
  ISBN 1-55583-627-5
  1. WELLES, JAN. 2. SINGERS—UNITED STATES—BIOGRAPHY. 3. WOMEN
BULLFIGHTERS—UNITED STATES—BIOGRAPHY. 4. BULLFIGHTERS—UNITED
STATES—BIOGRAPHY. 5. LESBIANS—UNITED STATES—BIOGRAPHY. I. TITLE.
CT275.W38115 A3 2001
782'.0092—DC21   2001033670
  [B]

CREDITS
COVER DESIGN BY MATT SAMS.
FRONT COVER PHOTOGRAPH OF JAN WELLES IN SUIT OF LIGHTS COURTESY OF
JAN WELLES.
FRONT COVER GLAMOUR SHOT BY MAURICE SEYMOUR, COURTESY OF RONALD
SEYMOUR.
BACK COVER PHOTOGRAPH BY BRUNO OF HOLLYWOOD.

Acknowledgments

A special note of gratitude goes to Lynn Diebold. She gave her time and expertise at the most crucial moments.

Also, a special thanks to Gary Davis.

My deepest thanks to Jo, to whom I am most indebted, for without her genuine encouragement I could not have relived this story. She gave me the heart to keep going. Therefore, this is dedicated to Jo and all the good people who helped me along the way.

To all the bad: You have taught me well.

$\mathcal{I}$ntroduction

From Broadway to the Bullring: A Toast to Our Stardust Girl

Never heard of Jan Welles before? You'll be glad you did. She's a dyke to watch out for—tough, gorgeous, tender, and honest. Her story takes us inside the world of show business—the business there's no business like—and back to a time (the 1940s and '50s) when celebrities were even deeper in the closet than they are now.

You could see Jan, in bouffant hair and Cinderella gown, every day on Arthur Godfrey's CBS morning show when the Old Redhead was the biggest thing in TV. She was his Stardust Girl—a tremendous voice with range and style who'd won his prestigious *Talent Scouts Show*. But it wasn't an overnight success. Jan had been singing professionally since she was 16, playing club after club in city after city, entertaining troops everywhere during the war.

But Jan Welles had a big secret. She was gay; she'd loved women since she was a kid in Pittsburgh and had always found plenty of them to love on the cabaret circuit. Leggy chorines, girl singers with the big bands, movie stars she met in plush New York apartments—they all pegged Jan for a butch under the makeup and frilly dresses and invited her up for a drink. She didn't disappoint.

South of the Border she was a smash hit too—with audiences and women. In Mexico she made it with one of Hollywood's biggest and brightest and gained more insight into the showbiz code. Everybody did pretty much what they pleased in bed, and the public was none the wiser. But if a producer, director, or any other old boy in power asked for a little nooky, a girl had to put out or forget about stardom. As Jan's famous female Acapulco one-night stand advised: "It goes with the profession."

Like all performers, Jan wanted to get ahead, but there she drew the line. Though she cultivated a girly look onstage, offstage she never denied her preference for women and never played the old boys' game. Even when that meant no Broadway debut and no $25,000 a week contract in Vegas. Maybe that's why you've never heard of her till now.

But Mexico changed her life in other ways. On a lark she accepted the challenge of the bullring—because it was, she said, a rare moment when that butchy person inside her could come out in public. She was a natural. *"¡Olé! ¡Torera!"* skeptical aficionados cheered when she fought brave bulls. And you too will cheer her passionate descriptions of hot blood staining blistering sand, even if she didn't like killing the bull (and she didn't).

So here she is, ladies and gents, our Stardust Girl in her "suit of lights." A toast to a long and glorious career of defiance, and to many more years of happiness with her girlhood sweetheart! For all gay people, that kind of happiness is the best revenge. As they say in Mexico, Jan, *"Salud, pesetas y amor, y tiempo para gozarlos."* Good health, wealth, and love, and time to enjoy them.

Lisa E. Davis
New York City, 2001

$\mathcal{O}$ne

God Bless the Child

It was Christmas Eve 1927, and the icy wind rushed through my sleeves. I looked at the red, chapped, gloveless hand that held mine, and then into my mother's eyes, and I knew she was cold. As far back as I can remember, I thought I was a boy, the protector of my mother. I rubbed her freezing fingers between my gloved hands. Smiling, she said, "It won't be long now, dear."

We were standing in a long line of people in Uniontown, Pa., huddled behind a Salvation Army truck, patiently shifting from one foot to the other as shoes were being distributed to the needy. Mama and I were among "the needy."

The people around us wore tattered coats and had rags tied around their shoes. At the age of 3, I didn't understand why my clothes were dark and shabby in contrast to the workers on the truck who were dressed in heavy overcoats, bright-colored gloves, and new, warm boots. Mama said the difference was a job.

It started to rain, so I moved closer to her to keep warm. She wrapped the bottom of her coat around me to keep me from getting sick like my father and sister Ruthie had. Two years before I was born, Dad had become ill with tuberculosis. Shortly thereafter, my 18-month-old sister died of the same illness. The pain of losing a child caused my mother to become overly protective of Dad and me. "Junie," she'd say, "put on your gloves." Then she'd turn to Dad with more orders. "Button your coat, Glenn, and get your hat." Dad would oblige, then I'd hear him clear his throat, hand me a pair of gloves, and say reluctantly, "Here, June. You heard the General."

Due to the highly contagious nature of my father's disease, I was sent to stay for a year with Mama's parents in Greensburg, Pa., in the house where I was born, on Reamer Avenue. Mama assured me that it was for the best, since Dad was so ill. Although many lessons are learned in a lifetime, those I learned while living with my grandparents have governed my entire life.

Grandma, a soft-spoken woman who stood about 4 foot 7 (she looked even tinier next to Grandpap, who was 6 foot 2), was meticulous in her practicality. Electricity was "too costly and dangerous," she said, therefore the house was equipped with gas jets that came through the walls; one jet hung over the kitchen table. And her clothing caused many an onlooker to hide a sympathetic smile. The hems of her dresses fell to her shoe tops, which covered her gray-and-red hunting socks. Sometimes she wore her shoes on the wrong feet, explaining, "Vell! Der only vorn out on vun site. Dare's a lotta goot left in um." A three-cornered shawl over her small shoulders was fastened at the neck of her dress with a mother-of-pearl brooch, the only jewelry she owned besides her narrow wedding band.

My grandparents had three girls and three boys. My mother, Enzie, was the baby. Money was scarce, and they spent what little they had for clothes on the oldest girl and boy. The next in line wore hand-me-downs. Mama, being at the end of the line, wore her brother Harry's old clothes.

Because of the extra hands needed for housework, Mama couldn't start school until she was 10.

"Anyhow," Grandma justified later, "it's more important to etch-a-cate da boys." To me that was puzzling and unfair. *Girls need to buy food and clothes too,* I thought.

As we sat and talked one night, I smelled wood burning in the huge black iron stove in the kitchen, and the aroma-filled air blended with the fragrance of chicory-flavored coffee.

Grandma's sunbonnets hung on a nail near the back door in the kitchen. Even though she never went out without one, her face was deeply tanned year-round.

Grandpap always stood with his shoulders back, which made him seem even taller than he was. He was a redhead with a red moustache and broad shoulders. I never saw him wear any color but blue: blue bib overalls and a blue work shirt, tattered but clean. His nickname for me was Rusty.

Mama and her sister Clara often talked about Grandpap's illness, calling it "hardening of the arteries." He'd sit for hours without talking, even when he was addressed. Then there were the times when he'd hit Grandma. On other occasions he'd take my hand and say, "Come on, Rusty, let's go up the street and play checks." And off we'd go, hand-in-hand, to the corner grocery, where there was always a checker game going on, and I'd stand by his chair and watch him play.

Bedtime was always a frightening time for me at my grandparents' house. I felt uneasy as I crept up the spooky stairway that led to my room. The stairs were on one wall of the kitchen—dark, narrow, enclosed, and steep. A gas jet at the top of the stairs only added to the eeriness. Trying to climb the high steps each night became an exercise in willpower.

One night when Grandpap had become violent, Grandma said firmly, "Chunie, go to bed, quick!" When I reached the top of the stairs, I ran to my room and listened. After much banging around that sounded like furniture breaking, Grandpap left the house. Minutes later I heard Grandma coming to my room. "Come wit me," she whispered. "I vont to show you something."

She took me to the room across the hallway and revealed

a concealed stairway with a little narrow door that was wall-papered to look like the wall. The opening was barely large enough to squeeze through, and I had to look hard to see it among the wallpaper design.

Grandma whispered when she told me about the hiding place. "If dare is effer trouble downstairs, if you effer get scared, go in dare und vait." Afterward I thought about the secret stairs sometimes at night, but at the time I didn't understand the meaning of her warning.

Living with my grandparents, I was constantly lonely and had no one to play with except Petie, the kid across the street. And I surely didn't want to play with her. We had settled our differences earlier.

One day, in looking for a playmate, I went to the front steps and waited for a girl named Jessie to pass by. It had been days since I'd seen her, and we had never been introduced. I waited a long time, then finally saw her walking from the streetcar stop with her mother. When I managed to work up the courage to say hello to them, they stopped at the front steps for a moment. Finally, the lady gently nudged the little girl's arm and said, "Well, Jessie, ain't ya gonna answer her?"

Jessie gave a slight sway to her body, leaned toward her mother's arm, and replied with a modest hello.

We were both about four years old. She was dainty and sweet, but most of all she was pretty. Her long blond hair hung every which way. Her eyes were soft, and she was always smiling.

Unable to foresee the impending disaster, I addressed her mother with a surge of confidence and asked, "Can Jessie come play with me after lunch?"

Too shy to answer, the young girl looked at her mother for guidance.

Realizing I had to gain Jessie's confidence, I continued, "My grandpap made a playhouse out of the old woodshed at the back of the lot. It has a linoleum floor, a little table, chairs, curtains, and a screen door with a hook."

Words couldn't express my happiness when Jessie said yes, she would come back later and play.

She arrived earlier than expected, before lunch, but that was no problem—none that I could see at the moment. After meeting her at the front steps, I took her hand and was proud to walk her past Grandma's colorful flower garden. Bunches of pink-and-white mounds followed the cinder walkway on the side of the house, making it a friendly-looking place. Grandma had spent hours digging in her garden, planting sticks under fruit jars and piling dirt around her rose bushes. She wanted it to be pretty for occasions like this.

Jessie relaxed her hand a bit as we reached the backyard. I pointed out the playhouse, and she skipped toward the screen door. On each side of the small house, vines of purple clematis that clung to the lap siding and continued their climb to the roof gained her attention. "How nice," she remarked, leaning closer to smell the flowers. I lifted the hook on the screen door, and Jessie entered the small room. Her eyes opened wide with excitement. Admiring the curtains and things, she said, "I sho-er do lak it." Then she seated herself in a chair and giggled, "I ain't never seen anythin' so fine."

I sat at the table for a while just asking questions. I loved to hear her answers simply because she had such a different way of talking. "We're from Booneville, Kentucky," she said. "My daddy lost his work so we up 'n' moved in with my mama's sister on Skidmore." She sure did talk different. Of course, I suppose our Pennsylvania Dutch sounded just as strange to her.

Jessie grabbed an imaginary spoon and pretended she was cooking on my cardboard-box stove with its crayon-drawn circles for burners. She placed make-believe pots on the stove and real toy dishes on the table. I remember wondering at the time what my job was. Surely I had one, but aside from looking at her I couldn't figure out what it was.

We'd been playing happily, chattering as kids do, when Grandma called. It was her "come to the table" call and that meant "NOW!" But what about my new friend? Would

Grandma feed her too? Was she even supposed to be there? And if I left, would she be there when I returned? I didn't want to lose my first friend.

"Wait for me," I said firmly. "I'll be right back." I latched the screen door from the outside as I left.

Running into the kitchen as fast as I could, I sat down at the table and had taken only a few bites when there came a wailing from the direction of the playhouse.

"Vhat on eart vas dat?" Grandma exclaimed.

I pretended I didn't hear it, but the noise continued. The look in Grandma's eyes compelled me to answer. "I guess it's my friend."

Grandma's small mouth tightened, and I saw her wrinkled chin jut forward as she said, "Vhat frient?"

"My friend Jessie, the one I locked in the playhouse so she wouldn't leave while I was gone."

Grandma yanked me from the chair and dragged me out of the kitchen, my feet barely touching the ground. The wailing grew louder and louder as we approached the playhouse. By the time we reached the screen door, Jessie was hysterical. From the sound of her piercing screams, she must have been terrified. Grandma unlatched the door, and in utter panic Jessie rushed past us, sobbing and shrieking as she ran down Skidmore Road.

"Vhat did you do dat for?" Grandma demanded, shaking my arm.

"I liked her and didn't want her to leave," I whimpered. "I just wanted a friend."

"Chunie, don effer do dat ag'in. Now, if she likes you, she vill come back!" Grandma's pointing finger marked every word. "You can't lock somevon in if day don't vont to stay. If somevon really vonts to be wit you, you von't need a lock. If dey don't, a lock von't keep dem. You remember dat."

That sad experience has remained poignant in my memory. After that, I spent most of my time playing alone, helping Grandma or looking for a new friend, because Jessie never came back. But I learned that if love is there, it needs no lock, no demands—it's just there. Another learning experience had occurred a few days earlier.

Petie lived across the street from Grandma. I can still see her coming down the long flight of steps in front of her house. It didn't take much to realize that Petie was a tough, mean kid. Whenever I'd wave to her, she'd make fists of her hands, straighten her arms at her sides, and march across the street to meet me, her immediate goal being to see me hit the ground. Once her goal was accomplished, she'd turn around and run back across the street and up the steps of her house. This happened a number of times, and I couldn't understand what I had done to offend her. Maybe she didn't like my red hair. Perhaps it was the way I was waving. But even when I stopped waving, Petie became furious. Seeing me always whirled her into action.

The next bout ended with cinders stuck in my knees. But Grandma was at the window and saw the attack. She ran outside, helped me up, and said, "Ven I get you cleaned up, you are going back out dere and giff Petie some of vhat she has been giffing you. If you don't, your bloody little knees vill feel vonderful compared to da vay your bottom vill feel after I get finished wit you." After picking the cinders from my skinned legs, she took me to the door and said, "Now go."

I didn't want to fight, but knowing I'd rather face Petie than Grandma's hand, I stood on the porch trying to muster my courage. After a few minutes Petie started toward me with her tongue out, thumbs in her ears, fingers wiggling.

That did it! She was the ugliest kid I'd ever seen! I crossed the street with my fists clenched and arms stiff, an imitation of Petie. Halfway there, I saw her eyes grow large and her mouth open in an O of astonishment. She turned and ran back, grabbing for the stairway railing leading to her house, her arms moving faster than her feet. I would have caught her, but the high-top shoes I wore in those days tripped me on the steps. I reached the porch in time to see the door slam in my face.

I felt a surge of mixed emotions: disappointment and pure satisfaction. Unsure of Grandma's reaction, I ran back across the street, yelling to her, "I'm sorry I didn't get her, but I tried!"

She gathered me in her arms, her comforting words holding a message and a lesson I never forgot. "You din't catch her, but you ver brave," she said. "It's not as important to fight as it is to stand up to it."

Many times I saw Grandma stand up to Grandpap, but she was no match for him. His violent behavior would stop for a few days and then for no reason begin again. One cold night, while snuggling deep between the feather ticks on my bed, I was enjoying the aroma of wood burning in the stove downstairs. I felt proud thinking of the firewood Grandma and I had gathered and the work we had done that day.

Suddenly it started: things banging against the walls downstairs, glass breaking, Grandma screaming. Then I remembered her advice about the stairway. Shivering cold, I slipped from the bed and ran to the pitch-black room with the hidden stairway. My hand groped the wall until I felt the seam in the paper.

Quietly I opened the small door and climbed onto the first step, pulled the door shut, and listened. The noise from downstairs was frightening. Furniture was being broken, Grandma was screaming, and I knew she was hurt. Huddled trembling in the blackened space, I felt utterly helpless. After a while there was silence, then I heard footsteps coming up the stairs. I couldn't stop shaking.

"Oh, please," I prayed, "please let it be Grandma." The creaking of the stairs stopped, and I heard "Rusty?"

Peeking through a small tear in the wallpaper, I saw Grandpap with a poker in his hand.

"Rusty," he called as he walked through the rooms. I wanted to bust out, grab the poker, and push him down the steps.

He kept walking...and listening...and walking, until his steps softly faded into silence and I sat listening to my own ragged breathing. Quietly I said every prayer I knew and perhaps a few nursery rhymes. I wanted to run to help Grandma, but I was afraid. Terribly afraid. I had been waiting a long time when I heard more footsteps. Someone was touching the wall by the little door. Holding my breath, I peeked through the tear in the paper. "Grandma!" I cried.

The door opened, and I heard "Chunie!" There stood my little Grandma with blood all over her face and dress, her hair stringy and wet. She helped me from the hiding place and held me close.

"He got that way again, didn't he, Grandma?" I cried.

"Yah, but everyting vill be all right after tomorrow," she whispered sadly. "Tomorrow ve go to da courthouse und tell dem 'bout Grandpap's sickness."

Shortly thereafter, my grandfather was committed to Mayview State Mental Institution, where doctors diagnosed him as criminally insane, caused by hardening of the arteries. Days later when we went to see him in the hospital, he was resting quietly. I couldn't understand why he had acted so differently at home.

Grandma, a pious woman and a staunch believer in God and the gospel, prayed for him every night. Still, she never went to church or took me to Sunday school, telling me, "You don haf to go to church to be a goot person." Then she'd add, "Your Grandpap is a goot person—he just has a sickness."

I lived in Greensburg until Mama wrote saying she had found work and that Daddy was well enough to care for me for the few weeks before school started. In June they finally came: Mama, Daddy, and Mama's sister, Aunt Clara.

Even though I was happy to see my family, I knew I'd miss living with Grandma. On hot days when folks walked by, she invited them to "sit a spell" on the shady porch, and then she'd send me running for root beer, lemonade, or water. Whatever she had, she shared. She taught me to be kind to every living thing. I learned to go to bed early, turn off the gas jets, get up early, start the fires, and be ready for a fresh day.

And although I was often lonely, I loved living with her. It was hard to say goodbye.

✳ ✳ ✳

The ride to Pittsburgh was exciting. Flaming-red coals shone on the mountainside, and the landscape became more and more awesome. As we neared our destination, the sky-scrapers looming over the city amazed me.

A week prior to our arrival, Mama was fortunate to have found us three rooms in a house for $15 a month in Fineview, just outside the city limits. The huge house stood on a steep hill surrounded by cinder and cobblestone streets, and tow-ered over smaller houses on either side. The front porch had spiral columns and fancy wood cutouts around the windows, which were dirty and black with soot from the factories. The landlady, who lived downstairs alone, was gruff-looking, with a red nose and wild, uncombed gray hair. As she glared down at me, I recognized instantly that she was a different kind of character than I had ever met. But as soon as she smiled, I saw a kindness in her eyes and knew she would be my friend.

A long flight of black steps on the outside of the house led to our rented rooms on the second floor. There were no flowers or vines or tomatoes, and the place lacked the warmth I had grown accustomed to at Grandma's. Inside we had no curtains, and the floors were bare except for a drab piece of linoleum in the kitchen.

The only furniture we had was a porcelain kitchen table, four chairs, and three army cots Grandma had given us. Still, water was piped straight into the sinks and we had a bath-room inside the house. Now that was different. We were together and that was all that mattered. And even though Daddy was in bed most of the time, his health was improving.

As soon as we moved in, Mama started her new job, hosing down freezer walls in a meatpacking plant. The owner was reluctant to give the job to a woman because the hoses were heavy and the job required working in freezing conditions and wearing rubber clothes. But he finally agreed to employ her at half a man's salary. Even as a small child, I wondered how it could be fair to pay one person more than another for the same job.

Every morning, after coming to my bed to kiss me goodbye, Mama left the house at 1 A.M. When she finished work, she'd return in time to fix breakfast at daybreak. On a warm day she'd walk 15 blocks to save herself the streetcar money.

The rubber raincoat she wore became ice-cold when she hosed down the freezer. For months she worked many hours each night washing and scrubbing ice from the ceilings, walls, and floors, then walking home in blizzard weather.

One morning Mama hadn't come to kiss me goodbye. I awoke to bright daylight reflecting off the white snow. Peeking in her room, I saw she was still in bed. I called to her but heard no answer. Tiptoeing in, I called again and patted her. Her hands and face were hot.

"Mama!" I called louder. When she slowly opened her eyes, I knew she was very sick, and Daddy was too weak to help. I ran downstairs for the landlady, knocked hard on the door, and told her about my parents. After a while she brought some soup and milk, and comforted them both.

Later that day the ladies in the neighborhood heard about our problem, and one by one they came to visit. Mrs. Williams brought sacks of flour and yeast. Mrs. Bickel gave us butter. Another brought soup. We were so grateful; it was our only food.

My mother struggled each day to get out of bed. She had to make do with what we had, so for days all we ate was some bread she had baked.

Mrs. Bickel, a lady who talked a lot to the other neighbors, stopped by one day. She was a round, pleasant woman who always looked neat in her clean dress and starched apron. This day, she came to visit while Mama's bread was in the oven.

To be in a kitchen with bread baking is to know the

enticing aroma and mouth-watering beauty of the loaves as they're tapped from their pans. The desire to cut into a hot loaf and spread butter on thick slices can be overpowering. Real home-baked bread is hard to resist, and Mrs. Bickel was an unexpected victim.

Would Mama bake a loaf for her? "Yes!" Mama said.

Pity must have nudged Mrs. Bickel into offering 10 cents for a loaf. Although Mama was still very weak, the next day she wrapped a fresh, golden loaf in white cloth for Mrs. Bickel. Seeing her about to head out in freezing weather, I warned, "You're sick, Mama. You wait here and look through the window while I cross the street. I'll be careful."

I felt a surge of pride as I marched up the walk through the snow, carrying a big warm loaf of bread. Mrs. Bickel gave me 10 cents for Mama and a penny for me for delivering it. She asked that Mama bake her a loaf every day.

Then a miracle happened. Mrs. Bickel told Mrs. Williams, who ordered a loaf every other day and two on Saturday, and that lady lived two doors from a "Monday only" lady. It went on and on. Mama would carefully place each neatly wrapped loaf in a long tomato basket. On every trip I managed to carry two baskets, and since Mama was feeling much better, she would always be at the window watching, and I would wave reassuringly.

After several weeks Mrs. Bickel offered me her grown son's red wagon. Scrubbed clean and lined with white cloth, the wagon could carry four loaves, the most Mama's oven could hold at one time. Our homemade-bread business was born, and with Mrs. Bickel spreading the word, news traveled fast. In fact, Mrs. Bickel should get credit for setting the price. After that first loaf, it was always 11 cents. The extra penny was mine.

As weeks passed, our customers increased from six to 15 to 30, new orders continually challenging my memory. Since I couldn't read yet, my only way of remembering was by associating one customer with another: The two-loaves-on-

Friday house was next door to the Saturday-only one, etc.

One day shortly after our bread business started, I noticed all the misters were home. I usually saw only ladies, but that day the men were in the street talking to each other while the ladies sat on their porches or stood at their fences talking. My first thought was, *It must be a reunion.*

I ran home to tell my parents about the commotion. "It's not a reunion," they said. "It's a crash."

The date was October 29, 1929, the beginning of the Great Depression. One by one the smokestacks of the iron and steel mills stopped spewing smoke. Our next-door neighbors, the Williamses, had to close their shoe shop since people could no longer afford to have their shoes repaired. Large and small businesses closed, and, as far as we knew, almost everyone in Pittsburgh was out of work except Mama and me. I was almost 5.

As I grew older and was allowed to deliver farther away from home, our business also grew. I sold bread to policemen at the shooting range on Union Avenue and pulled my wagon over cobblestone streets, up and down hills, four or five times a day in every kind of weather.

Many times I'd see my mother bent over the kitchen table, looking at the nickels and pennies she had pushed into little piles as she talked to herself: "This is for rent, this is for the doctor, this is for food," and so on. It was obvious that the doctor's pile was bigger than the others. "When I grow up," I told her, "I'll be a doctor. Then I can get you and Daddy out of this." Mama hugged me. I saw frown lines on her forehead, and asked, "Is everything gonna be all right?"

"Yes, June, but we have to keep going."

To me that meant if we worked just as hard every day, we could make it. We were partners in the struggle to get my dad well and keep our family together. I felt I could have helped more if only I weren't so young.

On school days the bread had to be delivered in the afternoon. My mother was baking 30 or more loaves of bread on a coal stove daily, and I delivered it Monday through Saturday—every day except Sunday, which was dedicated to church.

Sundays were awful. My secondhand shoes were uncomfortable—there was no telling who they belonged to before me—and the stiff, starched dresses made me look like a girl. My mother would wake me for church, and I'd give her every possible excuse for not going.

"Grandma told me you don't need to go to church to be a good person, so why do I have to go?" I'd say.

"Grandma didn't mean you didn't have to go to church," she'd answer. "She meant it wasn't necessary to go to be a good person. There's a big difference. You *are* a good person, but you have to go to Sunday school to learn about God and the Bible."

Mama would make me count out 10 of my pennies, with instructions to put them in the little plate at church. I questioned why I had to give up all that money, especially since it was so hard for me to earn. Mama's answer was never satisfactory.

At church the boys and girls were all in one group, except one Sunday when the teacher said, "I want all the boys to line up on my left and the girls on my right."

The children did as told, and I joined the group of boys. "June," she said, "you're in the wrong group. Come over here with the girls."

I quickly scanned the faces of the kids I was standing with and knew she was wrong. Perhaps she was confused because of my dress. If I were wearing my old coveralls, I thought, she'd know I was a boy. After all, what other difference was there?

Because of being asked to sit with what was to me the wrong group, I dreaded going to church. Finally, one Sunday, I couldn't stand it any longer. By the time I had walked to church, I decided not to go. Sitting on the curb, I watched the people going by.

"Mornin'," said the passersby.

"Mornin'," I replied.

Some were customers and recognized me. The boys were dressed in baggy little suits, supposedly to hide their knobby knees and bony shoulders. The girls looked fancy in their Sunday-best dresses with bows and lace. Although I was softer than the boys, I was much tougher and not as pretty as the girls. I kept studying the two kinds of people, the pretty ones and the rough ones. To me the only difference was that men—who were the laborers—were taller, stronger, tougher, and wore comfortable clothes. That was the group I wanted to grow into, but I still couldn't figure out why they called me a girl. They had to be wrong; they just didn't know it yet.

* * *

I had only one friend: Harry Snodgrass, a boy in my class. Harry and I walked to and from school together almost every day and went to a movie on occasion. Our friendship grew, especially since the other kids didn't hold a high opinion of either of us. They always called us names like "redhead" and "nigger," so I assumed they didn't like my red hair and they didn't like the color of Harry's skin.

Every morning as we walked to school, we'd pass a big yellow brick house where the Gananio family lived. Mr. Gananio, a bricklayer, had built it himself. A large sand-and-rock pile sat in front of the house, and a fine Indian cigar tree grew in the yard.

I never did get the count right, but there were a lot of kids in that family. After school I'd start out with my bread wagon and see the Gananio kids sitting on the sand pile smoking tobies, long pods from the catalpa tree. The smoke smelled awful. As I'd walk by, the kids would chant, "Yah, yah, Redhead, gotta sell your mama's bread!"

I felt everyone knew we were poor. This hurt, but the hurt and sadness turned into determination. I wanted to hurry up and grow so I could get my family out of this poverty. Still, it was difficult to ignore the children with their song and dance along my delivery route.

"Redhead, Redhead, gotta sell your mama's bread!" Those kids were pretty big. The little ones didn't smoke, but they all chanted.

One day as I came home from school alone, I saw the Gananio kids throwing rocks from their rock pile at an old picket fence. Walking closer, I spotted someone crouched behind the fence; it was Harry, huddled close to the ground, blood smearing the side of his face. I couldn't understand why they would throw rocks at him. He was friendly and never acted like the other kids. Running as fast as I could, I dashed through the side gate and ducked behind the fence next to him.

"Why are they so mad at you, Harry?"

He shrugged. "They just don't like my color!"

Who did they think they were not to like a sweet kid like Harry? I looked at the blood on his dark-brown face, and the sadness I felt brought out an anger I had never known before. Grabbing a handful of stones, I shouted, "Well, they don't like my color either, Harry! Come on, let's get 'em!" Gathering and throwing rocks from our side of the fence, we began a counterattack. "Just keep running and throwing, Harry!" I yelled. As we went through the gate hurling stones, getting closer to the sand pile, the kids took off for their house. But one of them was too slow. While Harry held him down, I shoved sand into his mouth until I was afraid he'd choke. When we finally let him get up, he took off like the devil was after him.

When we reached my house, I told Mama what had happened. Harry had nicks and scrapes, and we both were covered with sand. Only a mother could handle such a clean-up job. She grabbed a washcloth and gave us both a quick once-over. The wagon was full of bread, so I prepared to start my rounds.

"Will you be all right?" Mama asked.

"I'll be OK, but Harry's late getting home, and his mother is probably worried."

"I'll take Harry home and tell his mother what happened," she said.

Walking backwards, pulling the wagon uphill as I watched Mama and Harry go down the road, I felt rich for having helped a friend.

Harry and I became even better friends after that, and sometimes he would accompany me on my route.

"Don't you have any little girlfriends?" Mama asked one day.

"No. They're dumb. All they do is push their buggies," I told her. "They'll never amount to anything that way."

Although I didn't like to play with girls, I did like to watch them. When I wasn't working, I liked to study people, little ones and big ones. When I looked at childhood pictures of my grown cousins, they seemed to all look the same. Then, as they grew older, the girls became beautiful, and the boys looked unsightly as their faces broke out with fuzz and pimples. It was always the same. My mother wasn't beautiful, but she was prettier than Dad.

The only girlfriend I had as a child was Jessie. Once a month Aunt Clara took us to visit Grandma, and I'd look for her, but I never saw her again.

On one visit Grandma was excited because she had received a letter from Germany. Her cousin had written about a wonderful man named Adolf Hitler who wanted to change things and make the country a better place. Little did they know what was to come.

Many times on a visit to Grandma's, my aunt would take us to see Grandpap at Mayview Sanitarium, a sprawling building in the country. Upon arrival, we were instantly aware of the terrible odor of urine that permeated the building. In the lobby a woman directed us to a long hallway where the smell grew worse as we passed open doorways. As we walked through, we heard cries and moans from inmates, who waved at us. One man in white, the size of a wrestler, led us downstairs to a large open room. Inside were separate rooms with padding on the floors and walls, and fences at the doorways. Grandpap stood motionless inside one of the rooms. I had expected to find him in a hospital bed. A man in white explained that Grandpap was violent and abusive and that the family was afraid of him. Being too young to understand my family's fear, however, I could only feel sorry for him. Walking closer to his room, I waved, then heard "Rusty!"

"Grandpap!" I cried out as I ran past the attendant and put my arms into Grandpap's room to hold his hand. Calmly, Mama told me to let go, but Grandpap had a firm grip on my hand, and Mama spoke softly, not wanting to upset him.

"Rusty, I got a good job here," Grandpap said. "Every day I do the gardening. I'd like to go out and show you my flowers." Looking at the attendant, he shouted, "Open this door. I want to show Rusty my flowers." When there was no response, Grandpap became angry. He kicked, banged his head, and shook the fence. Finally, he stopped, came back, and held my hand gently. After seeing him lose control I realized why his room had padding on the floor and walls.

I wasn't afraid of him, but Grandma was, which was why she had the secret stairway in her house. But he had never hurt me, though it was frightening when he had gone after Grandma. Maybe he felt closer to me because we both had red hair.

After a long while Mama touched my shoulder and said, "It's time to go." My fingers slipped from my grandfather's deeply tanned and wrinkled hand. As we walked away, my eyes never left his.

Grandpap died in Mayview on September 15, 1931. He was 68. I was 7.

✳ ✳ ✳

About six years into the bread business, which provided our only income, our rent had been raised to $20 a month, with more increases on the horizon. We decided to move to a place for $15 a month on Union Avenue; it had four rooms and a gas stove in the kitchen.

My father's health had improved, and he was getting strong enough to look for work. Dad was proud and grateful when the manager of the Ritz Theater on Fifth Avenue hired him as a doorman. The job required little exertion and the pay was low, but he was working, which was the most important thing to him. When I heard my parents speak of the pay as being slim, I promised to help them when I was grown, although that seemed to be taking forever.

At the age of 10 I was placed on the girls' track team, and I became more convinced that something was wrong with me. I felt so out of place when I was around girls, but with boys it was entirely different. I could talk to them about anything and understand their way of thinking. I could also relate much better to my father than I could to Mama.

Many times I talked to Dad about my search for a profession. "Maybe I could be a doctor," I'd tell him. "I'd like to be a veterinarian. Dogs and cats are always following me along my route, and I help them when they're hurt."

The more I spoke of my decision, the more obstacles he'd mention. "What about the cost for schooling and the years of training? And besides, June, that's a man's profession," he'd say. The fact that a certain career was a man's profession didn't discourage me as much as the time it would take to learn before I could start earning money. Clearly I had to find something else to do.

I considered being a teacher, because I loved history. In class, Miss Vernon, a tall, thin woman with short light-brown hair, sat at the front of the class on a high stool. She'd talk for an hour about the Japanese aggression against China after General Chiang Kai-shek came into power. That was interesting to me, and gender didn't matter if you were a teacher, but how long would it take me to learn?

In searching for a profession I had to keep in mind that it couldn't require physical labor because I wasn't strong. I felt such confusion about my body; I didn't feel or act like a girl, yet I knew I wasn't a boy either. I was somewhere in-between, and I still harbored the thought that one day I would become a man. Perhaps when I grew tall and started growing fuzz on my face, everyone would find out the truth. It was a secret I kept to myself.

I joined every kind of sport offered at school to develop my muscles, and I always played with the boys. They were a bit rough at times, but the girls had such a gripping effect on me that I became dazed in their presence.

One girl in particular, Ellen, was beautiful, but I never spoke to her. I could only stand close enough to listen. All she ever talked about was the upcoming talent contest. It seemed that everyone at school was going to perform in it.

"What are you gonna do in the contest, Red?" Bobby Wocktel asked, laughing. "Pull your wagon?"

"Yeah, June'll sell some bread," the other boys joined in.

I knew they were just playing around, but it was embarrassing to think that Ellen might have heard them.

I had to think of something to do in the contest to impress her. I recalled Grandma saying, "You can do anything you make up your mind to do." And Grandma had never lied to me.

Almost everyone was entering the contest, which was sponsored by the Post Gazette Fair Play Club. First prize was 10 weekly appearances on Walt Farmer's Saturday morning radio show on WWSW. I thought of the child stars I had seen on the movie screen while waiting for my dad to get off work, and decided to take a lick at imitating them. Mama laughed— in fact, she almost cried—when I told her I had decided to enter the contest.

"What on earth are you gonna do?" she asked, as she continued laughing.

"I'm gonna sing, Mama," I said. "That's what I'm gonna do."

She smiled, trying to take away the hurt of her laughter, but it was too late. "You don't know how to sing," she said.

"I can try. I sing sometimes when I deliver bread."

My mother folded her arms across her apron, and I kept trying to convince her. "I've seen Bobby Breen and Nelson Eddy sing in the movies."

She tried to discourage me, to protect me from the disappointment I'd feel when I lost.

At school the ridicule worsened, even from the kids on the track team, who said, "Why don't you run in the contest, June? You're good at that." My determination just became stronger.

The next day I took 10 cents of my savings and hurried to the dime store for sheet music, where I chose the song "When Did You Leave Heaven?" I'd heard it a number of times on the radio, so I practiced it repeatedly until I'd memorized it.

The day of the contest arrived, but my mother didn't want to take me. "Junie, let's not go," she said, holding me by the shoulders.

"Why not, Mama?"

"Honey, you'll be so embarrassed."

"It's OK if I don't win," I said. "At least I'll be doing something."

Telling her not to worry, I set off with her for the Bellview Theatre: Mama in her long dress and me clutching the sheet music.

Backstage, a line of contestants waited their turn. Kids were planning on doing all types of things in the contest: singing, dancing, playing musical instruments. One boy whistled and another played the piano quite well.

When my turn finally came, I handed the sheet music to the pianist. He said he would give me an introduction, then I'd be on my own. I stood before the microphone as I had seen it done in the movies. I spotted Ellen in the audience and tried to imitate Bobby Breen's actions as I sang.

At the end of my performance everyone was clapping so hard, and smiling. The excitement overwhelmed me. I think I gave some part of myself to all those people, and though it was new, I felt a surge of pride and an instant rapport with the audience; perhaps it came from meeting people on my bread route, I don't know, but I loved the feeling. They kept clapping as I bowed and walked proudly offstage to Mama.

She was glowing. I had never seen her so happy. Backstage, after the last performer finished, we waited with the rest of the contestants and their parents for the judges' decision. Everyone was jabbering, and the next moment everything was silent. Then we heard the master of ceremonies announce, "And the winner is...June Walls!"

I had to wade through throngs of parents and kids to get out onstage. As I moved closer, the noise from the audience grew louder and louder until once again the bright circle of light followed me to center stage.

Some kind of magic was transpiring between myself and the audience. I sensed it and suddenly saw the whole world open up before me. At that moment I knew where I was going. They liked what they had heard. *This is what I can do,* I thought. *I just have to learn to do it better.* Again I was aware of the applause, and I took the lowest, grandest bow.

Backstage, Mama was smiling through her tears. She hugged me, and I was so excited, I couldn't stop talking.

"You know something, Mama, singers make lots of money. Why can't I do that, huh?" She remained wordless as she continued to embrace me. Excitedly I pulled away and looked at her, seriousness written across my face. "Mama, if I can just learn how to do it better, we won't ever have to be poor again." Without giving her a chance to speak, I continued, "Heck, if I can't be a doctor, I'll sing."

✳ ✳ ✳

For the following 10 weeks, as a part of my prize, I sang on WWSW's *Uncle Walt Farmer Show.* People who listened to the program said I sounded like Bobby Breen. Each week listeners called in requesting songs he had made popular, especially "Rainbow on the River." At Murphy's 5-and-10-cent store I picked out my favorite, "The Night Is Young and You're So Beautiful." Singing on the radio was exciting, but my biggest thrill came from performing before an audience. I relished the respect that came from my listeners; I had never experienced that before.

During that time a Saturday matinee in a movie theater consisted of a newsreel, a cartoon, a Tom Mix serial, and a double feature, and for a mere dime you could sit through the show as many times as you liked. I never missed a chance to catch the young stars like Deanna Durbin or Gloria Jean. I watched their movies over and over, and memorized their songs and actions. During my 10 weeks on the radio I pestered Mama to help me find a good singing teacher.

We heard about a vocal teacher who worked upstairs at the Ritz Theatre, where Dad worked. In the summertime the windows were open, and, in passing, I could hear students practicing. They had strong, operatic voices that could be heard up and down Fifth Avenue, even over the noise of the trolley cars. I wanted to sing like that and was certain the teacher had to be competent to have such talented students.

At last, one Saturday after the radio show, after Mama had caved in to my nagging, we hurried to the second-floor studio of the Ritz. The teacher was Lelia Wilson Smith of the New York Metropolitan Opera Company. Standing in the doorway, I heard a man with a powerful singing voice.

If I had been older than 10, I wouldn't have had the nerve to walk in and say, "I want to learn to sing." However, from the astonished look on Mrs. Smith's face when she heard it, I was sorry I had. She asked us to wait outside the studio until Peter Higgins had finished.

Twenty minutes later they emerged from the studio. The tall, robust man approached me and said, smiling, "So you want to learn to sing?" He bent down to talk to me, friendly-like.

"Yes, sir, I do," came my anxious reply.

"Well," he straightened his back and continued, "you're in the right place and in the right hands." Mama thanked him for the reassurance, and he left the room wishing me good luck.

It was 3 in the afternoon, but Mrs. Smith stood before us in a long evening gown. She was about 5 foot 8, weighed around 200 pounds, and had a very full chest. Her reddish-brown hair was combed into an upsweep in back. Her fingernails and lips were painted bright red, and her arms and hands were decorated with sparkling jewelry. Her black high heels with rhinestone buckles reflected tiny flashes of light at the hem of her dress as she walked. I had never seen anyone so glamorous.

In contrast to Mrs. Smith, my mother was stooped from years of hard work and donned a cotton housedress. I was embarrassed for her, but standing there I pictured Mama in an evening dress and fancy shoes and jewelry, and I wanted so much for her to have that someday.

The polished wood floor of the studio was covered with two large fringed rugs, with designs of peacocks woven into the border. Glass teardrops hanging from a chandelier in the center of the room reflected on light-blue velvet draperies that dressed the windows from ceiling to floor. Fine paintings in gold frames hung over marble-top tables, and autographed pictures of movie stars adorned every available space. My eyes grew wide with the startling glamour of everything; I felt like I was onstage in an opera house I had seen in the movies. Mrs. Smith told me to come to the piano and sing whatever music I had with me. I had chosen "Pennies From Heaven." Perhaps my choice came from wishful thinking.

When I finished, she looked pleased for a moment, but it completely deflated my ego when she patted my shoulder and said, "I only teach adults. A young voice can be damaged by beginning too soon." That was disheartening and meant I would have to wait until I was 16 before I could begin training for a job. I wanted to be working when I reached that age.

"But Mrs. Smith," I pleaded, trying to find the right words to change her mind, "young people sing in the movies, and they're studying."

Mrs. Smith was silent, so I continued. "I'm going to sing regardless. And if studying might ruin my voice, wouldn't not studying ruin it more? Besides, I really want to be good, and I'd do everything you ask. I promise. Please?"

Mama stepped in and humbly addressed the elegant lady. "Could you make this one exception, Mrs. Smith? My daughter has never in her life asked for anything. I want her to have this."

After a long pause and deep thought, Mrs. Smith responded, "If ever there is to be an exception, I suppose it should be with this voice." As she pointed her finger at me, I saw her diamonds sparkle. "If you agree to do exactly as I say, I will take you as a student. However," she raised her finger again, and with each downbeat of her words, the finger pointed at me, "if you do not, I will no longer teach you." As she folded her arms over her chest, I heard, "Do you understand?" She was tough, but I agreed enthusiastically and asked, "How much will it cost?"

"Let's start with a half-hour a week for $5. How's that?"

"Five dollars?"

The thought of my mother having to bake 50 loaves of bread to pay for one half-hour lesson was staggering. That was more than I made in a month. I was about to concede to the fact that singing lessons were out of the question when I heard, "Mrs. Smith, could I have a minute with my daughter?"

"Certainly," she said, and walked toward a door leading to another room.

Mama and I discussed it, and after some time she said, "I'll quit baking bread and find a day job if you can take care of yourself before school and come home at noon to fix your own lunch. That's the only way we can do it."

With no regard to the consequences and no thought of the fact that I had never been near a stove except for cleaning, I held Mama's hand and promised, "I will, Mama. You'll see. I'll study hard and practice every day."

I hadn't realized that Mrs. Smith had returned until I heard her say, "In the meantime, June, I want you to go outside every morning and breathe deeply, as deeply as possible, and hold it as long as you can. Start with 10 deep breaths and work up to as many as 20." I assured her I would start the next morning.

On the way home, Mama scribbled on a scrap of paper, trying to figure out how to cut corners and scrape together extra money for bills and lessons. I was so excited, I was hardly paying attention to her. I felt this was the beginning of a direction, and if I worked hard, I couldn't lose. Little did I realize the obstacles that lay before me.

That night I overheard a conversation between my parents. "But Glenn, she wants these lessons and the teacher must be the best. We heard her students singing and—"

Before Mama could finish, Dad interrupted. "My God, woman. Are you crazy? Work all day doing housework for $5 while she spends it in a half hour?"

Hearing him say this hurt me deeply. I understood that $5 was a lot of money, but we'd be doing it for him. Couldn't he see that?

"I don't care what you say, Glenn. June worked hard while you were sick, and this is the least we can do for her." Dad cleared his throat and was about to speak when Mama finished the discussion. "This is what she wants and I want her to have it. I'll look for work tomorrow." The General had spoken. Her decision to find work outside the home ended a business that had covered eight city blocks and served our family well for years.

The idea of the money being spent on my lessons, however, remained a constant thorn in Dad's side. It became something to quibble about whenever Mama complained about anything.

The first day that I had to fix my own lunch, I took the long way home, arriving five minutes before I was supposed to be back at school. Needless to say, I didn't eat. After that, I took the shortcut through the woods.

When the day finally arrived for my first singing lesson, my excitement grew from the moment I opened my eyes that morning until I ran up the studio stairs. I stopped long enough to smooth out the wrinkled $5 bill I'd been clutching in my sweaty hand, and after a gentle knock on the door, I heard, "You may come in." It was the crystal-clear voice of my teacher, Mrs. Smith. She looked elegant in her long evening gown, standing in front of a grand piano. She motioned for me to come closer. Then a finger pointed to a place beside her where I was to stand. She waited until a serious hush filled the room, and then she began. "Unless a voice is trained correctly, it will not endure. Damage is easily done to delicate vocal cords. You must treat your voice box as a valuable instrument. Therefore, at the first sign of a sore throat, do not sing. Do not practice. In fact, do not speak above a whisper." She was emphatic.

"Imagine a clothesline with many items hanging from it: a pair of socks, a sheet, a belt, all different lengths, but all starting at the same level. Now," she instructed, "think of the clothesline as the roof of your mouth, the hard palate. All notes must begin by first hitting the hard palate, whether they are high, low, soft, or loud." She put her hand on my shoulder, turning me to face her, as if to make certain I heard every word. "If you do not sing this way, you will never have a big, full sound. Regardless of how soft, loud, high, or low you sing, your notes must hit off the hard palate first." She reached for a glass of water, took a sip, and placed the glass on a coaster on top of the piano. Looking directly at me, she went on, "This is the way a singer attains a full, round resonance on all notes. Any other placement of a note will sound nasal, muffled, or swallowed." Then she directed her voice toward a doorway in the room, and pronounced, "Nora, we are ready to begin."

The door opened, and a lady not quite as tall as Mrs. Smith entered and took a seat at the piano. Her dark hair, pulled back into a chignon, gave her the look of a ballerina. She wore a black dress and no jewelry, which made the teacher seem even more glamorous. Nora ran her fingers over the keys. I was instructed to sing the scales, up and down, and back again. For half an hour all I did was sing scales.

So went my first lesson, and every one thereafter for the next six months. My time was devoted to practicing scales—no songs, just scales.

During those first six months, Mama lined up several jobs cleaning houses, but the thought of her working all day just to have me sing scales was frustrating, and I was growing discouraged. Finally, after six months, Mrs. Smith gave me my first song, "Neapolitan Nights."

"It has a challenging range for a beginner," she said. "The lyrics in this particular song will also allow you to achieve a solid sound." The lowest note in the song was F; the highest was G, below high C.

Our bread business had ended, but Mama's hard work was just beginning. Every day she left for work early and returned home at 5 in the evening. Dad was still holding his own in his job as a doorman. He was getting well, and as his health improved, his personality changed. Mama and I were becoming less important to him. I knew he was tired when he came home from work, but so was my mother. I'd hear them argue all the time about spending money on singing lessons. He'd lose his temper and start banging his fists on things, acting the same way Grandpap had. I was afraid he would hit her, and many times my fears were justified. I had seen this meanness in my grandfather, and I vowed to myself, *This will not happen to my mother.*

One night he hit her hard, and I saw rage in his eyes. An uncontrollable rage flew into my own body as I lunged at him with both fists flying, defending my dear mother, but we were no match for him. He pulled off his belt and beat us until we were whipped into the corner behind the stove, trying to protect each other. Then he continued the beating. He was turning into a maniac, and I hated him right then.

Bruised, cut, and hurting, Mama and I went into the bedroom and cried. She looked completely defeated, as though her world had stopped, but not mine—mine was just starting, with anger and determination. Soon I would be grown; soon time would be the equalizer. I had to get on with things if I was ever going to make it—and I would make it for her. Mama kept peace at home by skirting around certain issues, such as finances, hard work, or things she needed. Our cuts soon healed, but the mental scars remained, and I appointed myself as her ticket out of this kind of life.

* * *

Each day I practiced and continued with the breathing exercises, and everything was going well. Preparing my lunch at noon, however, was a trying experience. If I wasn't boiling the hot food over on the stove, I was spilling cold food down the sink or cutting my hand on a can or, worse yet, forgetting to turn off the fire under the food and finding the house full of smoke after school. I had no talent in that department whatsoever.

In fact, Mama never knew what to expect. One morning, after the house was filled with smoke, she called me into the kitchen. She had the table set for one. On the stove was a pan of cold soup with a spoon.

"June," she said, "all you have to remember is 'Gas On' and 'Gas Off.'"

"OK, Mama, I'll do it," I told her, though I felt extremely lacking at that moment.

* * *

The morning fog and smoke in Pittsburgh was so thick it would drift by in little dark clouds. You could taste and smell the smoky wetness. The cinder street was the long way to school, but the only way with lights. When I paused directly under one light, the next light was barely visible, but at least it was more than I could see taking the shortcut through the dense, uneven woods. I'd run up and down gullies, thick with trees and brush. The path was hidden and the fog surrounded me. Looking toward the ground, I could only see as far as the brass buttons on my coat.

By noon the fog had lifted enough to expose an irregular path through the woods. Each day I made the trip a little faster. I'd rush into the house, eat, wash the dishes, make sure I'd turned off the stove, lock the house, and take off running. I was turning into a deer in the woods, dodging low branches, making quick turns, and jumping over the creek. It was exhilarating. Between practicing my breathing exercises twice a day, scurrying through the woods, and running on the track team at school, I was growing quite strong and agile for my age.

One day about a year later, while hurrying back to school after lunch, I saw something in the distance darting in and out of the trees ahead of me. Then came a faint, familiar sound: "Redhead, Redhead, gotta sell your Mama's bread." It was the Gananios from my old neighborhood.

Three of them were laughing and dashing back and forth, singing, "Let's get the redhead!" I hadn't seen them in more than a year, and I knew I was in for something.

From the sound of their chanting, they were at least 50 feet away in several directions, surrounding me. I stopped, grabbed a fallen branch, and prepared myself for a fight. Suddenly they jumped out from behind their cover, each one armed with a stick. As the three moved in closer, they began to look shorter and shorter. Then I realized the kids were the same size as the last time I'd seen them, but I was looking down at the top of their heads. The redhead had grown.

I managed to grab one of the sticks and use it to knock the other two sticks from their hands. When they realized I was the only one armed, they turned and ran away. I never saw the Gananios again.

There was never a thought in my mind that there was any more physical difference between boys and girls than an outward appearance of strong and crude, and weak and pretty. Other than that, as naïve as it sounds, I never gave physical difference a serious thought. Mother never talked to me about sex, and there was no sex education in school. Therefore, the onset of my menstrual period, which began shortly after my 13th birthday, was the most traumatic invasion of my life.

If I had learned that every month a large horn would grow from my forehead, remain for a week, and return again the following month to continue the cycle month after month, I could not have felt more wasted as a human being. That day in school I felt nauseous, almost as though I'd faint at any moment, but with half the day over I kept fighting it off. On my way home, the light-headed feeling continued, until at last I made it to my room. Curled up on my bed, I had just fallen asleep when my mother called to me. "What's the matter with you? It's not like you to go to sleep in the middle of the day."

"I'm so sick," I told her, and it was even difficult to talk. "Pain, terrible pain in my stomach." I moved from the bed toward the bathroom. From inside, I called to her in panic. "Mama, I must have hurt myself. I'm bleeding."

After much effort, I made it back to my bed, where my mother explained what was happening. She talked for just 10 minutes, then stood to leave. I had never heard of anything so awful. In her short talk she only mentioned girls having this problem.

"What about Dad?" I asked.

"No, not men, but everybody has a cross to bear," she said. "Men have their problems too. Daddy has to shave every day. Now, how would you like to put up with that?"

I managed to say, "Shaving's not as awful as this is."

I couldn't imagine a more disgusting thing to have to contend with, to say nothing of the humiliating blow to my ego because of the filthy mess.

"Perhaps a doctor can stop it?" I asked quickly, as though I'd suddenly found a remedy.

Mama's eyes lowered as she muttered, "I think not." Then she left the room.

It was so unexpected. Before I had seen no reason to be concerned with how, or why, I was born. According to Mama, I was picked out at the hospital, and that was enough explanation.

I remained in my room for hours, confused. I tried to practice singing, only to find that the exertion required caused me to flood. I was shocked at the unfairness of it all. Why was I given this awful thing to hold me back? If this lasted for a week every month, that meant that a girl's accomplishments for a month must be done in three weeks. Lying there with my knees to my chin, I figured that one-fourth of my life would be taken away from me. I'd have to work extra hard to catch up to everyone else. Heck, I thought, I'd rather shave.

✳ ✳ ✳

In school I tried to be the best in everything, to win every spelling contest, to get the highest grades, because I had to achieve my goals in less time. Being athletic, I did well in track, the broad jump, volleyball, and after-school sports. But I never participated in indoor activities like basketball or gymnastics, because I refused to shower with the girls; I was embarrassed to have them see me undress.

On our volleyball team there was a girl named Rita. She was quiet, polite, and a good student. We often walked to and from class together, sharing opinions on school subjects. We'd also walk together gathering metal for the WWII scrap metal drives. The metal would be sent to England to help them prepare for war.

Rita's favorite song was the Andrew's Sisters' recording of "Bei Mir Bist Du Schoen." On my next visit to Greensburg I asked Grandma the meaning of the title. She said it was Yiddish and meant "To me you are beautiful." She also spoke of a letter she had received from her cousin Agatha in

Germany. "My cousin is 'fraid. She said de Chewish people are disappearink in Berlin. Whole families at von time, und everyvon is 'fraid to talk about it."

At the time the story meant nothing to me, especially since Rita was occupying all my thoughts. I'd look at her and say, "Bei mir bist du schoen," and she'd smile, not knowing what it meant. Her boyfriend, Jimmy, the local paperboy, was in the class ahead of ours, and Rita was fascinated with him. He looked ordinary to me, so I wondered what the big deal was. He had a job, but I'd been a wage earner for years. He was bigger, but I still had a lot of growing to do, and I had to do it in a hurry.

Shortly after seeing them together on one occasion, I realized I was growing extremely jealous over their relationship. Standing in front of my dresser mirror, looking at myself wearing pants and Dad's undershirt, I wondered what she saw in him. I looked thinner and my shoulders weren't as knobby as his—that part was good. Then I noticed two small lumps through my T-shirt. And that part was all wrong.

Rita wouldn't like that, because Jimmy was flat. But I could run as fast, my skin was softer, my grades were better, and he couldn't sing. So why did she go everywhere with him and not me?

One day Rita talked about a movie she wanted to see, then came the most difficult thing I'd ever had to do: I asked her to be my guest.

"Yes," she said, after calling her mother. "Let's go after school."

"OK, but first," I said, "let's stop by my house to drop off my books." Knowing there would be no one home at that hour, I was elated at the thought of us being alone. All the way home I walked with pride, feeling mature because I had a date with Rita, not understanding yet that she didn't share my feelings.

After arriving home, we went to my room to put my books away. Rita stood before my dresser mirror smoothing her hair.

"Do ya like Jimmy?" I asked.

"Sure. He's cute."

"Cute?"

"Yeah, June. Don't you think so?"

"Has he kissed ya?" I asked, trying to sound uninterested.

"Not yet." Then, picking up a small lapel pin from the dresser tray, she said, "Oh, this is lovely. Is it yours, June?"

"Yes, it's an angel. It was given to me at church. Do ya like it?"

"It's beautiful," she said, inspecting it more closely.

"Here, Rita," I said, extending my arm, "give it to me for a second."

She placed it in my hand.

Moving closer, I said, "I want you to have it." As I pinned it on her collar, she smiled, and I knew she was happy.

We stood looking at each other for a long time. Then I asked, "Can I kiss you?"

"Sure, I guess so."

I leaned forward and kissed her gently on her lips. She didn't pull away or seem displeased. We said nothing. Everything became still. The open space around us, our breathing—all was quiet. Suddenly I felt a unity with her that I had never felt before, like a ray of warmth and completeness. Slipping her hand in mine, I led her from the room with reverence.

I can't remember the name of the movie or what it was about. I can only recall the happiness I felt as I sat next to Rita, then as I escorted her safely home, and then the lightheadedness I experienced until I reached the privacy of my room, where I could be alone with my thoughts.

Days passed, then Rita asked me to join her at a football game, adding, "Jimmy's playing!" I was so hurt I couldn't speak. How could she do this?

"What do you see in him?" I asked, preparing myself for the sting of her reply.

"He's cute. All the girls like him. So why not? He's nice too, and besides, he likes me better than any other girl."

"But you're wearing my pin. Doesn't that mean anything to you? Doesn't that make us closer?"

Looking at me from head to toe, she answered, "How can I be closer to you? You're a girl!" After I heard those words, my head started to swim and a cold sweat came over me. I couldn't speak, so I just walked away from her. Returning home, I guarded the blow of my first rejection in secret. My hurt turned to sadness when I glanced at my washed-out Salvation Army dress and sweater. I wanted so much to swap clothes with Jimmy, to see how well he'd look in my old outfit. Surely that had something to do with her not wanting me. What other reason could she have? It was all so confusing. I knew I was beginning to look more like a girl all the time, but I felt so much like a boy that it was frightening.

Days passed and I turned my sadness into a determination to excel in everything. *I'll study harder at my singing and at school until I'm a success,* I thought. *That's what everyone wants—someone successful. So I'll do it, but not for myself, I'll do it for someone I care for, someone special. Then they'll want me, whatever I am.*

I wanted to talk to someone, but the only person who ever had time to listen was Grandma, when we'd visit her. And there were always so many people around that it was out of the question. Besides, she was worried about her family in Germany.

Hitler's army had occupied Austria and was now invading Czechoslovakia. As I sat and listened to this "insane horror," as they called it, my problems seemed unimportant. *Besides,* I thought, *that's crazy. Who would put thousands of people in an oven and burn them?* It was ludicrous, and I didn't believe it for a moment.

To keep myself occupied, I spent all my extra time practicing. My voice and diaphragm were becoming powerful, and I was hitting high C notes smoothly. The fact that my voice was high and feminine didn't concern me because I had a wide range, which meant it was also very low.

One day while waiting for a lesson, I heard Peter Higgins sing the classic "The World Is Mine Tonight." His voice vibrated the walls of the studio and gave me goose bumps. I wanted to have a big rich voice like his. "Please, Mrs. Smith," I asked, "could I sing a song like his?"

"No, no," she said. "That's a man's song. You sing this new one, 'Wanting You.' This one is for you."

His song wasn't just a man's song. It belonged to anyone who could sing it. There was nothing about it that I couldn't hit or sustain or color. Was it because of the lyrics, "The world is mine tonight"? *It's not just a man's world,* I thought.

Trying not to upset her, I did as told, but as soon as the lesson ended I went directly to the music store on Penn Avenue and bought the sheet music for "The World Is Mine Tonight." I studied the song, singing it inside my head all the way home on the streetcar. At home I practiced for a week until I felt ready.

The next lesson, I gingerly placed the music on the piano rack in front of Mrs. Smith. She was surprised, but her fingers sought out my key. Finding it, she smiled and nodded. One hand left the keyboard to point toward me, my cue to hit it, and I hit it with everything I had. When I finished, Mrs. Smith remained looking at the keys.

At last she raised her needle-thin eyebrows. "Not bad," she said. "Not bad at all." She turned on the piano stool to look at me. "Tell me, June, you'll soon be 14. Is that correct?"

"Yes, December 2."

"That was exciting, June," Mrs. Smith said. "You know I'm proud of how well you sang, even though you went against my wishes. You have the makings of a grand voice now, and it's developing rapidly. You're beginning to establish a style and feeling that are totally yours. However, you are studying to be an opera singer, and in opera you sing the lyrics as written, not as you wish." That, without a doubt, was the most gentle scolding I had ever received.

✳ ✳ ✳

The late 1930s were my early teen years, and I was a reasonable student in all subjects. Current events were most interesting, but I sometimes wondered if my interest was more for Miss Vernon than for her lessons. Weekly accounts of the war in Asia kept my attention as she sat half on the stool, with one toe just touching the floor and the heel of her other shoe hooked on the rung. She spoke of Italy joining forces with Germany, and Britain and France declaring war on Germany. "In Eastern Europe," she said, "Russian forces first invaded East Poland, and two months later they entered Finland." And Miss Vernon wore the tightest sweaters and skirts. "The whole of Europe is threatened," she said. Every day something new was happening in history class. I loved it and could have spent hours listening.

Mama was always at work when I returned home from school. She cleaned for wealthy people in Pittsburgh since we still needed two incomes to make ends meet. She was an expert at pinching pennies, and for this I admired her. Many times after seeing her tired from a long day, I'd reaffirm my vow to give her a happy life, a beautiful home, everything she wanted. Nothing could ever be enough for her. I also wanted to make up for the loss of my little sister Ruthie, who never had a chance at life. Perhaps I could succeed for her also, and my parents wouldn't feel so cheated. They wanted me to go out and have fun with people my age, not practice and study constantly, but life was serious to me and the kids at school seemed juvenile. There was so much to accomplish, so many things to learn. I couldn't waste a minute.

Mama, however, kept insisting that I meet socially with people my own age, so I finally agreed to go out. A nice German family we saw in church every Sunday, the Slemmers, had three children: Evelyn, Bobby, and Elliston, whom we called Al. Evelyn played the organ in church, and Mr. Slemmer and I sang in the choir.

The Slemmers were the ideal family. We went to movies and parties with them, to church, and to Al's baseball games. Mom and Dad liked Al, and I got the impression that his parents were working to get us together, but neither of us wanted that. We were good friends and simply had fun together. I liked to pal around with Bobby and Al, and I found Evelyn attractive. She tried to teach Al to dance, but since I had no interest in dancing, Al and I sat out the dances with deep conversations, planning what to do with the rest of our lives.

"As soon as I'm old enough," he said, "I'm going to join the Air Force. I want to fly one of those big bombers. That would be exciting."

"Yeah, it sounds exciting, Al."

"What do you want to do, June? Get married and have kids?"

"You kiddin'? I'm gonna sing."

"For a living?" he laughed.

"Yeah, for a living, and I bet you I'll be a success before you."

"Ha," he laughed. "OK, it's a bet, June."

Al was interesting to talk to because of his offbeat outlook on life. The most reckless thing we did was to drive fast to beat the curfew my mother had set. By 10 o'clock every night we went out, she would be standing on the porch waiting.

Her worrying was needless, though, because Al was just a friend. To me love was pure, simply a warm feeling for something beautiful: the bright eyes of a puppy, the sun shining through tall poplar trees on the hill—all these things were feelings of love to me and needed no further explanation. I saw all of this beauty in Rita, my first crush. Her voice and touch were like a warm breeze kissing my face. I wanted a closeness with her I couldn't explain. I loved being with her, and I never felt that way about Al.

On the Road

My daily jaunt through the woods at lunchtime continued. I had been studying voice diligently for five years, and Mrs. Smith encouraged me to take more lessons, at least an hour a week. Mother tried to give me the ordinary things needed for school and everyday living, but the thought of the added expense only caused more quarreling between my parents.

Arriving home from school one day, I saw my dad sitting at the kitchen table. I waved hello and started toward my room. "When did you get those shoes, June?" he asked, pointing to a used pair of saddle oxfords Mama had bought me. Before I could answer, Mama said, "I got 'em for her yesterday, Glenn."

"Yesterday, huh?" Then, holding his leg in the air, he said, "You see these shoes? Do you know how many years I've worn 'em? Do you? Guess."

"But Glenn," Mama said, ignoring his question, "June outgrew her old ones."

"Ten years, that's how long."

"For God's sake, Glenn, you've been in bed for nine of those."

"Ten years."

As usual, an argument followed. Over time, my father

disapproved of nearly everything Mama did on my behalf.

Knowing I was the point of contention between my parents, I felt getting a job might help. It would bring in extra money and get me out of the house, which would hopefully eliminate the arguments.

Dad spoke with the manager of the theater about a cashier opening, and Warner Brothers agreed to train me as a relief cashier. I was only 15, but I learned the job quickly. It was a challenge to handle the long lines of people waiting to buy tickets, but I enjoyed being sent to all areas of town to pinch hit for cashiers who were sick or on vacation, or who had phoned in last-minute excuses for not working. They called me the "baby of the circuit" because of my saddle shoes and bobby socks, but I had fun and made money.

On one occasion I was sent to the Enright Theater in East Liberty. When the late-night cashier failed to show to relieve me, I was asked to stay on until 11 P.M. Because of my age, I wasn't supposed to work that late, but in this case I had no choice.

After closing, I waited for a streetcar, which were few and far between at that hour. The theater manager came by with a friend who, after speaking of the late hour, offered to drive me home. Considering I had already been waiting 45 minutes, I was grateful. He seemed like a nice person, neat and clean-cut, so I thanked him and we started off.

I lived on the north side of town and knew the main streets from the streetcar rides. Once out of that area, however, I was easily lost and had only a general idea of which way to go. When I pointed out the direction we should be going, he said calmly, "No, there's too much traffic."

Leaning back, I relaxed, content that he knew a quicker way. After all, he was no threat to me—he was just a kind person. But before long, nothing looked familiar.

"I'm sure you're going the wrong way," I remarked, looking out the window.

"No, I'm not," he smiled. "It's OK."

After miles of silence, I sat listening only to the wind rush past the car and the clicking sound of a pebble that had become embedded in one of the tires.

"Where are we going?" I asked. Then, pointing over my shoulder, I said, "I live back that way!" Again there was no answer.

The clicking of the tire came faster as he accelerated. I stared at him, but he kept his eyes fixed on the road ahead. His face seemed to have changed; it appeared ridged, stone-like, intense. He gripped the wheel hard, guiding the car over roads unfamiliar to me. My muscles tightened. Knowing nothing except good and bad, sane and crazy, I thought, *He's trying to scare me.* The odometer continued to roll, and an inner voice told me something was wrong with him. I'd seen that look in my grandfather, and the same red tightness in the face of my dad.

I prayed for a stoplight, but none came. My heart pounded as I shrunk deep into the car seat. How stupid I'd been to accept the ride. I'd been warned about strangers. I was turning crazy with fear. *I'll have to fight for my life,* I thought. *He'll try to kill me.* I was gasping for breath, losing control.

We were on the outskirts of town. There were no house lights, and traffic had disappeared. The car swerved. He made a hard right turn onto a narrow, bumpy path that ran through a wooded area. He continued driving recklessly through the woods until finally, hitting the brake, the car came to an abrupt stop.

Then he grabbed me. His hands were like iron. I twisted free from one and was caught by another. My dress ripped. I fought for my life with fists and feet. He grabbed one arm. I lunged for the door handle with the other. His fingers dug into my flesh. With both my feet on his chest, and pressing my back to the door, I moved my back to release the door handle and pushed with all my might, calling on everything in me to defend myself. As the door sprang open, I twisted free from him and toppled out of the car. Quickly I groped along the ground for anything I could use as a weapon.

Grabbing a large jagged rock, I stayed crouched in the shadow of the open door. When my assailant rounded the front of the car, I became the attacker. Clutching the rock in my right hand, I gripped the door handle with my left for leverage. With a surge of terror and adrenaline, I smashed the rock into his face. I heard a sickening squash, like the sound of a melon splitting. He groaned. Listening, afraid to breathe, uncertain how long the blow would stop him, I turned and ran for my life.

Blindly I ran, afraid to pause for an instant for fear that he would catch me. The woods were so thick, but I was used to this, and I prayed to God he wasn't. I bobbed and wove through branches and brush not knowing in which direction I might be headed. Blood roared in my ears. An inner voice commanded, *Run, run.*

I heard snapping twigs and sticks behind me. Certain he wasn't far behind, I ran as though I were one step ahead of hell. My strong ankles carried me over unexpected rocks and limbs on the ground. Through the thick brush I spotted a dim light in the distance. I turned, making my way through the thicket, and headed straight for the light.

At last I saw a house through a clearing. I ran as fast as I could, screaming, "Help! Please help me! Please!" The door flew open. Hysterically I fell into the arms of an elderly couple. They led me inside, and the lady sat with me. I was freezing cold and shaking uncontrollably. She covered me with a quilt, then held me gently, quietly, as I slowly tried to recover.

Loading his shotgun, the man rushed to the door. "Please," I warned, "don't go out there. He's crazy." Disregarding me, he opened the door and took a long careful look into the darkness.

The police were called, and when they arrived, the officers wrote their report. They said they would drive me home, but I wasn't so sure about them either. I was afraid to trust anyone. They phoned my mother, reporting to her that I was all right.

The officers drove me home, where Mama had a hot bath

waiting. The first sane moment I had was when she sat on my bed and spoke to me as though I were a small child, telling me not to worry because I was safe now.

As days and then months passed, I never heard another word about that night. No one mentioned it again. It was as though it hadn't happened, or they had all forgotten—everyone except me.

The incident instilled a bitter lesson in me. I swore to myself that I would never again be in a position where I had to rely on a stranger for transportation. From then on I would always be in control of my travels. It was a lesson I learned the hard way.

✳ ✳ ✳

As my studies with Mrs. Smith continued, my voice developed into a mezzo-soprano. I had mastered "Un Bel Di" from *Madame Butterfly* and Mozart's "Alleluia," and I sang at weddings and funerals. Finally, at age 16, I was capable of hitting G above high C.

I had been studying to be an opera singer, but when Mrs. Smith explained how much more training it would require, I knew I had to settle for less to meet my family's immediate financial needs.

Although I gave my paycheck to Mama each week, it wasn't enough to allow my parents to quit working. Dad had recovered but was incapable of keeping a well-paying job because he tired easily. My mother worked constantly. Over the years I had often spoken about the home I would buy them someday. If I were to keep my promise, I had to get started.

In 1940, at the age of 16, I was offered my first professional singing engagement at the Seventh Avenue Hotel cocktail lounge for the dinner show. I explained to my mother how difficult it would be for me to work and keep up with my schoolwork, and that if I couldn't keep up, I would fail. I was certain it would be better to quit than to stagger through. This required a lot of convincing on my part and much deliberation on hers, but she finally gave her consent. It was, however, a decision I later regretted.

The Seventh Avenue Hotel had a revolving stage with a piano and an organ. I chose to perform "The Donkey Serenade" and songs from popular light operas, such as Victor Herbert's "My Hero" from *The Chocolate Soldier*. I selected several other ballads and asked for Mrs. Smith's help. She taught me how to add color, meaning, and softness to a popular song. I was accustomed to classical music, which doesn't give a singer a great deal of flexibility. With popular ballads I could render my own interpretation. Mrs. Smith guided my phrasing and breathing in the correct places, and I learned how to give the lyrics special meaning. As I was leaving my last lesson, she held my hand, and I will always remember her words: "You have the voice now, June. The rest is feeling."

I put together a repertoire and an act I believed to be entertaining. My only major problem was what to wear, since all I had were skirts and blouses. I asked my mother to pick out a pattern and material and make me two long dresses. It was a good thing they were long, because the dress had to cover my saddle shoes, the only shoes I had.

I broke my act in at the VFW and the Moose and Elks Clubs to smooth out the rough spots. At last I felt like a professional singer.

After my run at the Seventh Avenue Hotel, Dad got me my first agent, Margaret McLaughlin, whose office was in the Ritz Theatre building. We met, and she agreed to book my act and get me started.

Margaret booked me into the Monte Carlo and other clubs around Pittsburgh. Then I began to travel to small towns close to home. On the train I tried to appear worldly and adult, even though it was hard to keep track of my luggage with such excitement. I knew enough to tip the porters and cab drivers. *No one will know I'm only 16*, I thought. *I'll have them all fooled.*

After arriving at one of my first clubs, I asked for the

manager, too green to know he wouldn't be there in the afternoon. Little did I know, there was no need for a welcoming committee. For a rehearsal, you need the band, not the manager.

I was shown to a dressing room and realized instantly that dressing and undressing with other performers was going to be a problem. In school I had refused to shower with girls in gym class because I had felt uncomfortable. It was simple back then. Dad's doctor had always warned mother about having me bathe and go directly outside. A cold settling in my lungs would make me more susceptible to contacting tuberculosis. In school I had a written note from a doctor. Around grown women, though, I knew I'd be like a 16-year-old boy.

Regardless of what I looked like, inside I was still a boy who was expected to dress and undress with a bunch of beautiful women, and it was frustrating as hell. A fast-moving show meant quick three-minute changes for some acts. One of the acts would finish a number, the dressing room door would fly open, I'd hear, "Holy shit," and some gorgeous woman would rush in with a whole vocabulary of words I had never heard before. With hands full of a feather headdress and various parts of a costume, she'd turn her back zipper to me and say something like, "Get me out of this fuckin' thing!" and off it would come. Until then I'd never known that dancers didn't wear panties under their costumes; they wore strings attached to a little V. Finding this so interesting often made it difficult for me to concentrate on my reason for being there.

My first big club date came along, and on the bill was a line of 16 dancers. The dressing room was long and narrow, and along the walls were individual chairs and dressing tables with a mirror encircled with lights over each one. I sat at one end of the room, feeling like a hayseed in a flower bed. I got the feeling after the first night that they recognized my tendencies and wanted to embarrass me just for the fun of it.

Nine girls were each sitting at a dressing table when I heard the "five minutes to show time" call. The girls asked one another if anyone had seen the rest of their group. "They're gonna be late," someone remarked. Suddenly the door opened with a bang and in rushed seven young women breathing heavily. Street clothes started flying everywhere and everyone was shouting across the room.

One girl yelled for her "goddamned eye pencil!" Another one broke a "fuckin' strap" and asked for a pin. Next to me stood a nude girl searching frantically in a makeup kit. "Where the hell's my razor? Who the hell's got my razor?" Through the rubble of lipstick tubes, Max Factor grease paint, and such, she found it. Then, with one foot propped on the table, she put a mirror between her legs and began to shave. My God, I not only saw it, but it was magnified.

My eyes grew wide with disbelief. "Oh my," I said, then turned away. I couldn't stand it any longer and still be able to keep my mind on singing. I felt a compelling warmth all over. I broke out in a sweat and tried not to look. But I wanted to see.

Rushing from the dressing room, I went to the manager and asked for a private place to dress.

"Why?" he laughed. "You think you're a headliner?"

"No, sir, I don't, but please could—"

"What do you want, a star on your door?"

"No, sir," I said, "it can be a half-moon, I don't care. I just want out of there!"

As I recall, the manager let me use his office as a dressing room. After that, there were other club dates where I dressed between cases of beer or whiskey, or between two sheets, but always alone. I made sure "private dressing area" was written into my contract.

✳ ✳ ✳

Every week I sent money home to my mother and dad. At first I wanted to stay close to home, but then I was booked for two weeks at the Valparaiso Inn in Florida.

"June, that's too far from home," Mama said. "I can't let you go."

"But it's the only way I can make money. I can't just work in and around Pittsburgh. The agent won't be able to get my salary up."

Dad seemed to be around when it counted. "Look, Enzie," he said, "you wanted her to learn to sing. Now let her sing."

They saw me off at the station in Pittsburgh. Mom was still wishing I'd change my mind, but again Dad and I convinced her that travel was necessary to make the kind of money I needed to help them out.

In Valparaiso, the star of the show, "Simone, the Silver Goddess," was a dancer with an unusual act. Her body, the most flawless arrangement of curvature I had ever seen, was completely covered in silver paint. A silver skullcap covered her hair, and she wore silvery china-silk wings attached to the back of her neck, arms, and onto the ends of three-foot-long buggy whips she held in her hands. The vision was one of a mythical human butterfly with huge iridescent wings.

Before the opening of the first show, the manager informed me that Simone, being the headliner, would be the last act. The painting of her body had to be timed so that it wouldn't stay on more than 10 minutes. If her pores remained covered longer than that, she could suffocate. That meant I could do no encores.

After my act I watched Simone perform. In preparation, the house lights went out, and she had to make her way to the stage in total darkness. We heard the introduction to her music, and as the black lights came on, she was posed onstage with her arms stretching the silver-blue wings to their fullest. My eyes held a steady gaze on her body as she moved to the music, and I felt teased and embarrassed by a feeling of reverent worship. I was floored.

On closing night, before her number, an electrical problem held up her act 10 minutes. When she finished, she rushed through the crowd backstage and grabbed my arm in passing.

She could hardly breathe. "Help me! Please! Come with me!" she panted. "I'm burning up!"

Together, we ran to her dressing room, where a large trough filled with water sat. She ripped off the cap and the silk wings, and lowered herself into the water. With both hands she scrubbed herself frantically and immediately sighed with relief. Paint floated around her and ran in streaks over her breasts, hips, and thighs as she stepped from the tub. I stared and felt frozen to the spot. I took quick, shallow breaths to control an irresistible urge to scream, "My God, you're gorgeous!" Tossing me a towel, she said, "Here, get my back!"

I started wiping while she tried to clear the paint from her face. As I wiped, she turned. I wiped her side, her waist, her hips. As the towel moved over her flawless skin, I tried to touch her with the side of my hand and became aroused. After her body was dry she thanked me, and I said, "Glad to help." She had no idea how glad.

* * *

In 1941, Margaret booked my act into Saks Show Bar in Detroit for my first big-city appearance. Again Mama went with me to the station. Again she waved goodbye, hoping I'd change my mind.

The train arrived in Detroit in the morning. I checked into the Hotel Detroiter, just off Grand Circus Park, bought a paper, and got settled. Detroit was the nation's fourth largest city, and I felt I had made it to the big time when I saw the ad for the show in the *Detroit Free Press*. The star that week was George Gobel, and there would be a chorus line, a dance team, and a master of ceremonies.

Rehearsal was set for 2 P.M. I asked the desk clerk how to get to Saks Show Bar by streetcar, figuring that would be a lot easier on my pocketbook than taking a cab. So, carrying a music case and gown, I rode the streetcar to the club. Inside the club I busily tried to take in everything at once. The stage was enormous, with colored footlights and overhead lights. This was my first experience working with a big band, and they sure knew how to play. I had to sing extra loud to keep up. *Wow,* I thought, *if Miss Smith could hear the way this orchestra plays my music, she'd be thrilled.* I worked hard that afternoon and had never sounded better.

When I finished the number, I looked at the band. They were all smiling, and I wondered if they played like that for every singer or if they were trying to drown me out.

After rehearsal I returned to the hotel to prepare for my first night. My throat felt a little rough, but I decided it was merely opening-night jitters.

During my first show, the band and I worked hard, and the audience was fantastic. I sang "Chapel in the Moonlight" and "This Love of Mine"—the only songs I had with me—so the second show was a repeat of the first except for a wardrobe change.

My voice was big, so I stood at least three feet from the microphone. When the horns behind me began to blare, I was too inexperienced to move closer to the mike; I just sang louder. The audience responded. At the end of the last show my throat felt as if it were closing up. Much of it was from nervousness and worrying about being in a big show for the first time, although a good part of it could be accredited to my trying so hard.

After the show, around 3 A.M., I heard a knock at my dressing-room door. I opened it to find one of the line girls still in costume. "Hi!" she said. "Are you the singer that's causing all the ruckus?" She was about 5 foot 4, blond, with lovely brown eyes, and was wearing a sparkling outfit.

I opened the door wide to let her in. Not knowing what to say, I announced, "I've got a sore throat."

"Well, it doesn't sound that way."

Her name was Penny Westman, and it turned out that we were staying at the same hotel. She invited me to join her and the rest of the dancers for a streetcar ride home, and I jumped at the chance. I needed a friend to get my mind off my nervousness.

Boarding the streetcar, we passed the crowded front section and moved to the back. As we took our seats, several line girls and dancers joined us. Most of the people in the front of the car were cheap-looking. Girls were dressed in short, tight, low-cut dresses and wore stale, reapplied makeup, and the men hanging onto overhead straps were groping them. I couldn't hear the conversation, but from the loud giggles, glances, and the bumping of their hips as the streetcar stopped, they appeared drunk. This was my first glimpse of city nightlife.

During the ride, my throat felt worse, which I mentioned to Penny.

"Do you have something at the hotel you could take?" she asked.

"No," I told her, failing to add that home doctoring was my mother's job.

"Well, that's no problem. The hotel drugstore is open all night. You can get something there."

I hadn't planned on getting sick so soon. Little did Penny know I wouldn't have the slightest notion as to what was needed.

Entering the lobby of the Detroiter Hotel, she pointed to the pharmacy to the left of the lobby. I nodded, grinned, and kept walking toward the elevators, too embarrassed by my lack of knowledge in that department.

Trying to appear mature and in control, I went to my room. After I changed into my old flannel pajamas, the phone rang. It was Penny.

"Well, what did you get?" she asked.

"Ah, well, ah, I thought I'd wait until morning."

"And what if it's worse by morning, then what?"

I had never felt more stupid, and it was a relief to hear her concern.

"Listen," she said, "will you drink some hot lemonade if I bring it?"

"Sure, but you don't have to." All the while, I was hoping she'd insist.

"I'll bring you some. Just open the door when I knock."

Five minutes later I heard a tap at the door, and Penny stood in the hall bearing packages. "I bought some lemons and mustard," she said as I let her in. She stopped upon entering, looked at my long legs poking through the too-short pajama bottoms, and burst out laughing.

"Where, pray tell, did you get that sexy outfit?"

I glanced down to get the overall picture, and my feeling of worldliness shattered. As embarrassment heated my face, I wondered how an adult would reply.

"Say," she said, cocking an eyebrow, "just how old are you anyway?"

It hurt to have someone ask, especially when I'd been away from home for only 24 hours.

"Sixteen."

Penny howled with delight. "You mean that tall, sexy gal who wowed 'em at the club tonight is just 16? A 16-year-old brat, that's what you are. Now it makes sense. No wonder you're so quiet and don't answer questions. You don't know what to say, do you?"

"I guess not," I mumbled.

"First we'll get you well. Then tomorrow I'll show you how to put on stage makeup, and we'll see how they go for that." Hands on her hips, she added, "My God, it's just my luck to run into a 16-year-old kid who needs help."

Penny wetted a towel with hot water and packed it with mustard. Then she gave me several glasses of hot lemonade. After that she told me to lie down, and she slapped that messy stuff in the center of my chest. The sweating began.

"Are you afraid to be alone on your first night in a big city?" she asked.

I wondered how she could tell. It must have had something to do with my speechlessness. I didn't want to admit that just knowing a friend was there would be my total salvation.

"Well, answer me! Would you like me to stay with you tonight until you're better?"

I couldn't force myself to answer, due to the turmoil going on inside me. I wondered if she knew my secret. I wondered if she also recognized something different about me. Something even I didn't understand.

"Well, ah..." I started, still speechless.

"OK, I'll go to my room and get something to sleep in."

"Thanks a lot," I managed. "Knock and I'll let you in."

"No, no, you stay warm. I'll take the key and let myself in. I'll be right back."

Penny seemed to know what to do about everything, so I went to bed and relaxed. I was about to fall asleep when I heard the key in the door. She had come back as promised.

As Penny walked around the room, I could hardly believe what I was seeing. She was wearing some lacy little thing, the kind I had seen in the movies, only thinner, even see-through. I kept watching. It was the first time I'd been in a bedroom with such a mature woman who wasn't my mother.

She was so sexy, and I was lying there hiding behind my mustard plaster, sweat, and flannel pajamas. Her figure was beautiful, like Simone's. As she walked around the room, her breasts jiggled, and I wanted to reach out and touch them. If she knew what I was thinking, I thought, she'd probably run like hell.

After a few moments she slipped into bed. The lamp was turned out, and I lay there like a board, unable to relax. In the blackness of the room, she smelled so heavenly that I wanted to move closer to her. As I inched my way to her side of the bed, the fragrance of her perfume seemed to escalate my fever. My head and chest were pounding, and my fever turned to chills. I felt the same exciting sensation as when I had touched Simone. I began shaking and was short of breath.

"What's the matter?" Penny asked. "Why are you shaking?"

I couldn't tell her I wanted to touch her. I was in agony.

Trying to cover up what was going on, I said, "I don't know, but my fever is going everyplace. Something strange is happening. Maybe you should call a doctor."

Penny turned on the lamp and looked at me through lovely, soft eyes. "Have you been with anyone close like this before?"

"I've never been this close to anyone."

"Have you ever kissed anyone?"

"Oh!" That remark only added to my problem. "Well, I kissed a girl once."

Penny remained calm while I struggled to control my breathing. "Did she respond? Did you like it?" she whispered.

"Oh, yeah! I mean, yes, I guess."

"Do you have a boyfriend?"

I told her about my friend Al.

"Did you ever kiss him?"

"Oh, no. He was like a buddy, someone to talk to, that's all."

"Was there anyone you were attracted to?"

"Yes, but I've got a problem."

"What kind of problem?" Penny asked with an understanding smile.

After a long pause I mumbled, "I'm different."

"In what way? You can talk to me, June."

"Well, at school one of the fellows said, 'A lot of boys like you, June. Just take your pick from those who pick you.' His remark disturbed me. Those who picked me, I didn't want, and those I found myself looking at surely didn't want me. In fact, they didn't even know I was standing there feeling confused."

"How were you confused?"

"The way I look..."

"What about it?"

"Well, it's not the way I feel on the inside," I said. "I often wonder, *Does anyone know I'm in here?* I don't have anyone to talk to. So I have to be truthful with you, Penny—I'm not what I look like on the outside."

Penny switched off the lamp, and the blinking neon sign outside the window cast shadowy designs across the bed.

With each moment of darkness I inched closer to her. Silence surrounded us, except for the soft sound of the moving sheets and my pulse pounding in my ears.

Penny put her arm around me and took my hand, placing it on her breast, then pulled me toward her, and we kissed gently. She raised her body and directed my lips to her breast. She then slipped her leg between my thighs as she tenderly guided and welcomed my feelings of affection. She sighed with pleasure, and her pleasure ignited a progressive force within me, through my body and into the direction of her touch until I exploded.

"Whew!" I cried out and rolled to the floor on my knees. "Oh, oh, please. I have such a cramp! Oh, please."

Penny slipped out of bed and knelt beside me. As the neon sign flashed off and on, I saw her smile and heard her whisper, "Come on, you'll be all right. Let me help you into bed, and I'll tell you all about it. Come on."

"Wait, please," I begged. "Just let me sit here a minute. I'd better not move."

"Is this the first time that's happened?"

"Oh, yes."

"But we barely touched."

"Oh, I know, but I couldn't stand anymore. Will it ever happen again?"

"I certainly hope so," Penny said.

"Does it happen to everyone?"

"If it doesn't," she said, helping me back into bed, "they're missing the time of their life."

We talked for hours. I found her lovelier than anything I had ever known. For the first time I knew the pleasurable pain of all that beauty. Finally, we drifted off to sleep.

* * *

The following morning the entire world looked different, not complicated or confused. But all too soon we had to return to the club for our evening shows.

That night I sang love songs with a new feeling and understanding. The audience was seeing one thing, but they were getting much more. The two-week engagement ended too quickly.

The next booking was in Springfield, Ill. Penny decided to take a week off to visit two friends, Lee and Carol, in Chicago. "They'd love to meet you," she said, "and they'd be able to answer more of your questions." Seeing my interest, she suggested I take a train with her to Chicago, stop over, and then go on to Springfield. I agreed.

When we arrived at Union Station, we were greeted by an attractive lady in her early 40s wearing a light-blue suit. Her dark hair was streaked with premature gray on either side. Penny excitedly hugged her and introduced us. As Carol reached for my hand, her winning smile quickly told me I was welcome in her big city and accepted as a friend. She and Penny apparently were very close and had a lot of catching up to do, for they kept the conversation going in the cab en route to the apartment. Looking out the taxi window, I was thoroughly impressed with the magnitude of Chicago.

Once inside the spacious living room, which was tastefully decorated in pastels, I was introduced to Lee, a tall, handsome woman of great poise and character. She was direct in her movements but quite ungraceful. Her mannerisms reminded me of myself—not at all feminine. Lee and I shared an instant rapport, a kind of harmony.

That evening we enjoyed a candlelight dinner and adjourned to the living room for coffee and conversation. That's when the many fears, feelings, and questions I had about myself were answered.

"There are many homosexual men and women in the world," Lee told me.

"Men too?" I asked.

"Sure. Penny's brother Cliff is gay. He was stationed in the Philippines. And one of her uncles is too. There are many of us. You've met them, but you haven't recognized them because their voices are silent. They don't demonstrate or display their feelings in public."

"Why can't they be honest?"

"Because of repercussions and ridicule from people who don't understand." Lee leaned toward me. "I'm the vice president of one of the largest banks in this city. Do you think I'd remain in my position if it were known that I don't do the same things in the bedroom as other people?"

"What does your bedroom have to do with banking?" I asked.

"I suppose it has to do with society's lack of knowledge on the subject. You'll be hated by many people who don't understand."

They were kind to me, and I was grateful to them for their honesty. They explained the slang that was connected with homosexuals. "We're all called 'queers,'" Lee remarked, "and the men are called 'fags,' but don't ever stoop to the level of the person who calls you a name."

"Lee, can I ask you something that's very muddled to me?"

"Certainly, June. What is it?"

"OK," I began, "I may be asking a dumb question, but I have to ask. If I'm attracted to women, why aren't I attracted to all of them?"

"We're no different than heterosexuals," Lee explained. "Opposites attract. You're very masculine or 'butch,' and Penny is 'femme.' That's why you two are compatible, but you can't categorize anyone by their appearance. A masculine-looking woman may be quite feminine after you get to know her, and the same holds true with men."

I confessed to them my relief at knowing I wasn't the only person in the world who felt as I did. They accepted me the way I hoped my mother would eventually, but with my mother it would take a lot of explaining. Also, if she found out before I turned 18, she could make me live at home until I became of age.

After talking to them, I now had a clear, panoramic view of life. I was not like everyone else, but with this new awakening,

I realized that being different didn't make me wrong, it only made me who I was.

The next morning I thanked them as I was leaving, and Carol said, "Remember, June, some people will say you're wrong and claim that this is your choice. You and I know we have no choice—our feelings are genuine. So, above all, be true to yourself."

On the train to Springfield I felt less troubled, less alone. There were many people who were just like me. I could smile with an inner peace, feeling for the first time that I had an identity of my own.

*t*hree

Good Morning, Heartache

One Sunday morning in a New York hotel, I was just getting dressed for breakfast when I heard a commotion from outside on the street. "Extra! Extra!," voices were yelling. "Read all about it!" Over and over they shouted. Half asleep, I went to the window and heard, "Japs launch sneak attack on Pearl Harbor. Read all about it!"

I quickly finished dressing and ran downstairs to buy a paper. In a nearby diner I found a stool and ordered a glass of milk. I looked around and saw that everyone was reading the newspaper. As I scanned the first few lines of the top story, I couldn't believe what I was reading.

At 7:55 on Sunday morning, December 7, 1941, the Japanese had launched 350 warplanes and 28 submarines in an attack on Pearl Harbor. Five American battleships were sunk, leaving 2,400 Americans dead and 1,179 wounded.

People at the counter were talking to strangers next to them. At the club that night it was the same way; the mood had changed and everyone was stunned.

The following day, December 8, Japanese warships shelled Guam and Wake Islands, and on that day, Japan declared war on the United States and Great Britain. That evening at the club the mood had changed again. The war had come to the United States, and now we were angry. Never had a declaration of war succeeded in uniting a country and its people behind their leader as had the events on this December day in 1941.

I had been 17 for all of five days when the attack occurred. Suddenly every citizen was motivated into helping the country in whatever way possible. Wanting to do my part, I phoned home to ask Mom and Dad's permission to join the WACs. The thought was devastating to them, so I asked if they would sign to let me join the United Service Organization. The USO, established by six major charitable groups, helped keep up the morale of U.S. servicemen and women and was funded through monetary donations and volunteerism. I had been performing at Army, Navy, Marine, and Air Force bases for several months, but I wanted to do my part overseas. Mom begged me to dismiss the thought, having already lost one child.

My parents became frantic at the possibility of losing me, so I volunteered to do as many performances as possible for service people in the States. I performed everywhere they needed a show, at benefits of all kinds and in hospitals, sometimes 10 or 12 shows a day. I sang at canteens in every town I happened to be in and at Sheepshead Bay whenever I played New York. The GIs were so appreciative that they made a better performer out of me, and singing for them was a pleasure. Men in uniform were everywhere, and I made friends with many of them.

One evening while working the Bluegrass Room at the Brown Hotel in Louisville, Ky., I was asked to perform at the officers' and enlisted men's clubs at Fort Knox, and for the patients at Nichols General Hospital. I felt privileged for having been asked. The following weekend the Bluegrass Room was packed with servicemen and women, and ladies in evening gowns. Between shows I was invited to a table of two couples of service people. Betty, a WAC, introduced me to Florence, another WAC, and to Ken and Robert, both army sergeants. After the usual questions—"Where are you from?

How long will you be in town?"—they asked if I had a boyfriend or if I was married. I told them no, figuring I might as well be truthful.

If they turned and ran, I'd be seeing their true side. So I said, "I prefer dating women." Directing the conversation toward Ken and Robert, I continued, "No offense, fellows, but…" and the four of them started to laugh. I wondered what was so amusing. "I knew it!" remarked Florence, an athletic-looking woman. "By damn, I told you!"

Florence stretched her open hand across the table, palm up. "Sergeant," she said, "pay up." Her fingers continued to wiggle until Robert laughingly placed a $5 bill in her hand.

"Boy, June," he said, "you had Ken and me fooled. I thought I was pretty good, but you don't look it, you know."

Betty, who was extremely attractive, gave a radiant smile as she said, "Florence and I knew you were 'family,' June, just like us."

Relieved, I said, "It's so good to be in your company."

Checking a watch, I noted that it was time for my last show, and they promised to come back the next weekend.

The following week they returned and were seated at a table of eight, all "family." We had another few hours of good conversation and laughs. I had great respect for them and was envious of the job they were doing. To wear a uniform and fight for our country was a privilege, and I felt cheated that I couldn't do more.

During the war years, the government distributed ration stamps, and even the simplest things were hard to come by. Leather virtually disappeared from stores, as all available material was needed for boots and gear for servicemen. Man-made shoes came on the market in bright colors and high styles, but I heard it wasn't unusual to have a pair fall apart if you were caught in the rain. One dollar could buy a pair of ankle straps or platforms in any bright color, but I found it next to impossible to find a pair of comfortable low-heel everyday leather shoes, and that's all I wore.

Patriotism was never rationed, though—that proud, lump-in-your-throat warmth. We all had it. Music and shows dazzled with American pride. Jobs of all sorts flourished. Factories and mills rolling at full tilt manufactured goods for the war effort. Before the war, nearly every home with two incomes had some sort of domestic help. But when factories started offering top wages, maids in middle-class homes became a luxury of the past. Everyone was willing to do whatever they could for their country.

While singing for audiences of service people, I began getting requests for pop music that I couldn't handle. Switching from singing classics to ballads—and learning to deliver a song with emotion—required outside help. I heard about a qualified teacher in New York who had coached Frank Sinatra; perhaps he could help me. He wasn't a vocal teacher, but a stylist with whom I could learn—or unlearn—breathing and phrasing.

His first advice after hearing me sing was, "Don't sing the whole song with only two breaths. Break it up into short phrases. I don't care to know what you can do. I want you to learn what you *should* do."

"You have a strong voice," he told me. "But that's not important. Many a gravelly voice has turned on an audience if the singer feels the song. Feeling, that's what counts."

After six weeks of training, I accepted a two-week contract to work the 51 Club on 52nd Street in New York. It was a hole in the wall, but because it was next door to the Onyx Club where Billie Holiday was appearing, the engagement became the most valuable two weeks in my career.

Billie and I both did three shows a night, and mine started a half-hour before hers. After each of my shows, I'd run next door to watch her perform. The Onyx Club was jammed nightly, and 8x10 glossy photographs of Billie were plastered out front—that was impressive. When opening the front door, you saw only the backs of people, and once inside, you could hardly move. I introduced myself to the hatcheck girl, who gave me a standing room in her booth where I watched each performance nightly.

During the introduction of the show, while the pianist's fingers rambled over the keys, there was a hush in the room. Then he leaned toward the mike and distinctly enunciated, "Ladies and gentlemen, Billie Holiday!"

All heads turned in the direction of the front door where she arrived with her entourage. And all eyes focused on the sultry lady making her way through the network of people who had come to see and hear her. Then, with dignified elegance, Billie would step onto the small platform and begin her mesmerizing.

I studied her intimate way with the audience. She had a close rapport with people that made them crazy for her, and yet when she walked on the street, drank from a fountain, or rode on a bus, she was met with discrimination.

Her artistry opened my eyes to what an audience wanted. They didn't care how high or full a voice was, or how long a note could be held. They wanted the intimacy of it all.

A strong voice was necessary in a large room or theater, but in a small club a singer's delivery had to convey more of a delicate union with each person. Billie Holiday was an artist who had mastered her trade, and I changed my style after watching her. She was beautiful both in performance and appearance. Always being awkward as a kid and growing up with nicknames like "Copperhead" and "Red," I'd never felt pretty or, heaven forbid, sexy. That was how I saw other women, not myself. After seeing Billie perform I felt I had to make up for my lack of "looks" by being a skilled entertainer.

My agent had been asking for 8x10 glossy photos for several weeks. Seeing Billie's pictures in front of the Onyx Club made me realize how important they were. At the time I only had one picture, and it looked like a yearbook photo. So I made an appointment with Maurice Seymour, a photographer well respected among entertainers for his lighting effects. I took the two dresses Mama had made and went to his studio.

Mr. Seymour was a small man, and he kept busy doing something or other every minute. Looking at me from all directions, he began moving lights to get different effects. He asked me to sit on a bar stool in front of a screen and then continued moving lights. I was asked to stay in uncomfortable positions, while he kept clicking his camera, saying, "Look here." (Click) "Chin up." (Click) "Shoulder up a little, not too much. Close your eyes." (Click) This continued for an hour.

A week later the proofs were spread out, and I was awestruck.

"That's me?" I asked, wide-eyed.

"That's you!" Mr. Seymour confirmed.

I couldn't believe it. The photographs showed a woman— a sultry, sophisticated woman. That didn't fit me. I wasn't like that. Not wanting to hurt his feelings, I said as tactfully as possible, "They won't know who I am."

"Why not?"

"Because I don't look that way. I mean, I recognize the dress, but I'm not that, uh...you know."

"I only photograph what I see, and you may not think of yourself as 'that, uh, you know,' Miss Walls, but you are! You're just not used to seeing yourself this way."

Even though the photographs were stunning, I felt like a phony. Mr. Seymour picked out the most professional shots since I was at an absolute loss.

Later, when the pictures were ready, I studied them and realized I'd better start looking and acting like the woman in the photos. I could imagine the disappointment of a club manager who'd been expecting that sexy-looking babe in the pictures if I came bungling in with slacks, sweater, saddle shoes, and a ponytail and no makeup.

After I went shopping for street clothes and dressier flats, my agent suggested a different style of gown to work in, something clingy. Until that time I had only worn long flouncy dresses over low heels. With a slinky gown, I'd have to wear high heels. Since I was pretty clumsy, my biggest concern that first night was making it from backstage to the microphone at center stage without stumbling. If I could get that far, I could handle the rest.

✳ ✳ ✳

Things started happening quickly. I began getting new jobs with my new style and new look. It was a joke. Everyone thought of me as a sexy chanteuse, while I felt more comfortable in Dad's undershirts. I was the same person, but the outside wrapping was a guise of glamour, and few knew what was inside.

Onstage, a pause to gain composure—nonchalantly glancing at the floor, raising my head, or pushing a strand of hair from my face—brought attention. Men started gravitating to me. They were everywhere. I'd find myself flanked by two of them making cutesy remarks in the club, and I'd stop and tell them honestly, "You're wasting your time, fellas. I like women." Walking away, I'd glance back smiling. It was always the same; they'd look at each other with their mouths open. I had such fun with that remark and have always wondered why I didn't get clipped. They probably didn't believe me.

Everyone was telling me my songs were sexier now, but they were the same songs. My visual metamorphosis attracted a different type of audience, one more interested in the outside wrapping of the package. I grew more determined to try to override the façade by being recognized as a good entertainer and nothing more.

My determination led me to many towns and cities. Traveling along, I saw homes with small white satin flags in the window, each one with a blue star in the center. Each flag honored a person in that family who was serving the country. Some windows had five or six flags.

In those early years of my career, I worked every little town in the eastern half of the United States where there was a night club or service club. Some towns were merely specks on the map, but they all had floor shows, and that was all that mattered.

I kept searching out the USO Clubs and working. *Keep working,* I thought. *Keep money coming in.* Anything more than what covered my expenses was sent via money order to Mom and Dad.

My career was going smoothly, and I was booked into a little club in Johnstown, Pa. On the show with me was a solo dancer from New York by the name of Ruth Clay. She was also a redhead, the Susan Hayward type, and had the kind of beauty that holds one charmed at first sight. Immediately I wanted to know her—at least that's how it all started. I had the opportunity to see Ruth's work nightly because her routine, which was set to the "Warsaw Concerto," preceded mine. The music featured a stirring melody that allowed one to feel the beauty of Warsaw before the September 1939 German invasion, then experience the sorrow of the people of Poland after their surrender. The music was mystic, and Ruth Clay moved with graceful artistry.

The third night, after I finished my act, Ruth was waiting backstage. She gave me an intense look followed by a smile and then a warm "Hello, June. I'm Ruth."

She asked if I'd like to join her for a "night lunch." Feeling immediately at ease in her company, I said I'd be delighted.

Traveling alone, I had often missed hearing a friendly voice. Two-week stands left little time for developing friendships, so tonight I was eager to change into street clothes and hurry to the nearest lunch counter.

We finished eating and left the restaurant at 3 A.M. The streets were empty, so we walked. As Ruth talked about the show, the war, and her music, she appeared to enjoy my company as much as I enjoyed hers. She was full of questions, but I had none for her. Everything I wanted to know was there beside me, and I was dazzled!

There weren't many hotels in Johnstown, and, as chance would have it, we were both staying at the same one. As we entered the small elevator, she turned to me with a smile. "How about coming up to my room for a drink? Whatever you'd like! A Coke or a cocktail?" Of course I agreed.

Leading me to her room, she kept the conversation moving. Lucky for both of us, for had I opened my mouth, I would have exposed my inexperience, as I had with Penny Westman. Eagerly I walked with her down the hallway, feeling like a 14-year-old boy.

Once inside her room, she handed me a small container for ice. "Do you mind?" she said. "Just go downstairs and ask the desk clerk."

Back down the elevator I went, then into the lobby. The night clerk took the bucket and sauntered through a swinging door. When he reappeared, I thanked him for the ice, and returned to her room.

The door opened, and I saw Ruth with a different look, bathrobe tightly wrapped and tied and her hair falling over her shoulders. The room was small; a bed, nightstand, and straight-backed chair were the only furnishings. Ruth folded a pillow under her head as she lay on the bed, while I tried to get comfortable in the chair.

"Tell me about your life," she said. Up to that point, there wasn't a great deal to tell. But I quickly answered her questions, mentioning happenings and acquaintances, and briefly spoke of Penny.

"Penny?" she said quizzically. "I sense there's something special about Penny." She patted the space on the bed beside her. "Come over here. Come over here and tell me all about Penny. You need to talk, June. The most I've heard from you is your singing."

Ruth made me feel comfortable, so I confided in her. "Penny is the only person I've been with," I said.

"You mean you've never been with a man?"

"Why would I want to do that? I want the same things they do." I sat up straight in the chair and waited for her next question.

"What does your family say about your being a homosexual?" Ruth asked.

I felt uncomfortable at the thought, but I answered her. "They don't know yet. When I tell them, I want to tell them in person, and then they'll understand."

Ruth was flirty, and I was so green that I used every diversionary tactic to keep from talking about lovemaking. She touched my arm with her fingertips, beckoning me to lie beside her. But I kept the conversation flowing by changing the subject because I didn't want to make love to her. She had never been with a woman; maybe I wouldn't be what she wanted. Perhaps she was merely curious. I didn't want to be with Ruth just to satisfy her curiosity, so we just sat and talked for a while before I went to my room.

All during that next week, I watched Ruth's act and was thrilled by her smooth ease of movement. I admired her ability, her stage presence, her music arrangements, and her warm smile. She was frivolous but fascinating.

After the last show of the engagement, Ruth asked me to join her again for a late-night snack and then invited me to her room. "Come on over," she said. "Be with me. I'm going to pack a few things and we can talk."

By that time I'd become a bit more relaxed around her. She went to her room while I stopped at the desk for ice. I got off the elevator at her floor, ran down the hallway, and paused abruptly in front of her room. I straightened my back and pulled myself together. *Hot damn!* I thought. *Most guys would have to put on a tux to get this far!*

When the door opened this time, Ruth had candles burning on the dresser, and a radio played soft music. Her mood was different, as if all of this were a sensual strategy. As she packed her bags, I was aware of her thoughts being elsewhere: Clothes were tossed in, then removed, then tossed in again. I knew she was much too seasoned a traveler to pack in such a manner.

After a few minutes she snapped the locks on her luggage,

tilted her head, and said, "Now, just who do you think you're fooling with that innocent look?"

Caught off guard, I said nothing. I wasn't exactly innocent, but then I wasn't very experienced either, so I just sat there and tried to figure out what to do next.

"You're so shy, June, but I like that." Soft strains of a beautiful melody were playing on the radio. Ruth began to dance slowly, seductively, each movement beckoning this novice until, coming close to me, she pulled me to my feet. When I became a part of her movement, awkward as I was, she whispered, "Do you know what I want?"

Ruth's passionately playful ways were like an alluring magnet moving me about. Moments later the enormity of my desire overwhelmed me, as she guided me toward satisfying her. She was quite a teacher. I felt so mature; women like me were everywhere, easy to find, I thought. It was a relief to know she had seen through all of my glamour, sequins, and paint.

The following morning, as she prepared to leave for her next club date, Ruth turned to me. "Your mother must be proud of you," she said. "Do you call her often? Would you like to call her now? I'm sure she'd like to know how well you're doing."

Since I sent all my extra money home, I usually wrote letters, I told her.

"Come on. I'll place the call. What's her number? I'd like to say hello."

Ruth was bubbling with excitement. In all innocence I thought, *How sweet of her to do this,* not thinking this was a strange request with perhaps an ulterior motive. She placed the call after I gave her the number in Pittsburgh, and the two of us talked to my parents for several minutes.

Ruth gave me her address and phone number in New York and was insistent on my promising to see her again.

Six months later I was booked into a club in New York City. As soon as the usual drag of finding a room and checking in was over, I received a call from Ruth. She said she had seen the ad for the show and had called every hotel until she found me. How flattering. *I must have been pretty good,* I thought in my own cocky way.

Ruth sounded happy to talk to me. "I have a surprise for you," she said, without giving me a clue as to what it was. "Come over as soon as you can."

Anxious to see her again, I rushed to bathe, dress, and flag a cab. My look of achievement must have covered me from head to toe as I ran up the stairs of an old brownstone on the East Side of New York City.

I rang the bell and a delightful voice asked "Yes?"

"Ruth, it's me, June!"

I waited. The lock clicked, and through the curtain covering the glass in the door, I saw a silhouette.

Ruth peeked around the partially opened door and smiled, but the smile quickly faded. Stepping into full view, she slurred a quick "Surprise!" and there she stood.

"My God! You're pregnant!" I stammered.

It was beyond my comprehension how anyone so willing to go to bed with me could switch to men and allow this to happen. What a blow to my ego.

Her apartment was clean and efficient, but very dark—as dark as her mood. She said she had married and that the baby was due in five weeks. Recovering from my initial shock, I responded, "Well, congratulations."

With both hands she waved off my well wishes in disgust. "I was in love, so I got married," she said.

"Then why are you so sad, Ruth? You should be happy."

"It didn't work out. He was a son of a bitch."

She busied around preparing coffee, and we talked for a while with no mention of the love affair or the baby, just show-business talk and good times. We had a few laughs, and then I decided it was time to leave.

I called for a cab and was about to go when Ruth solemnly said, "June, I need your help. The point is...I need money."

"Money from me? Why me? Where's your husband?"

"Who knows? Like I said, he's a son of a bitch. But I do need money to have this baby. I need $550, and you can see," she said, adding a comical arabesque, "I can't dance for it."

"Ruth"—I felt my jaw tense—"I send every penny, after expenses, to my parents. I don't have any money to give you."

"Please don't say you don't have it," she practically begged. "I need it. I don't want to do this to you, June, but I'll be forced to call your mother and tell her what you are and the way you've been living. I don't want to, but I will to get the money. I'm desperate!"

The muscles in my neck tightened as I listened to Ruth's well-planned entrapment. The baby was due in five weeks. I had been with her six months earlier. That's why she had been so aggressive with me—she was already pregnant. I felt a sick burning in the pit of my stomach. To me our time together had been special, and I felt deceived. I left quietly, telling her I'd call later. She gave me one week to get the money to her, and I knew I had to do it. This wasn't something I could tell my parents by phone, and I couldn't have them hear it from a stranger. I knew Mom would accept any choice I made as long as I was happy, but I had to be the one to tell her.

The more I thought about Ruth, the more I saw her true colors. That day in the hotel room she had insisted on placing the call to my parents so that she'd have the number.

I'd been trying to save for the house I had promised my mother and father. I was also saving for a car. With the accumulation of luggage, a new wardrobe, music, photos, and street clothes, having my own means of transportation was essential. And there were many clubs I couldn't work because they were situated on the outskirts of a town. Now, because of Ruth, the car and house would have to wait.

It was difficult to believe that people would stoop so low, but I was learning. Women weren't just beautiful; some were dangerous. Boy, was I learning.

By watching my money closer than ever the following weeks, my savings recovered from the dent made by Ruth.

Deciding I had enough cash on hand, I arranged my work schedule to spend a few days at home. I was still afraid to tell Mom and Dad about my life, because I was only 17.

The most important thing on the agenda while I was home was getting a car. With no regard for the fact that there was a gas shortage and that tires were next to impossible to get, I went on my merry way.

In Pittsburgh, Dad, Mom, Aunt Clara, and I visited one used car lot after another. The third day a red Plymouth convertible with a white top caught my eye. Mom didn't approve of the color, but it was sharp! Real sharp! I bought it. That was the first of many cars that followed. Still to come were a Chevrolet; Buick, Chrysler, and Lincoln Continental convertibles; a Buick station wagon; and a Swallow Doretti sports car, but with this first car I felt so grown up. What a laugh. I thought I had been through hell and back and was so wise. I thought I knew my way around but had no idea that this was just the beginning.

With the family waving at the curb, I was on my way for my first solo drive. I went directly to my old high school. Why? For all the years I had been shunned for being poor? For being different? Who knows. But my plan was to arrive when school was letting out, park in front, and wait. Perhaps their heads would turn now. Perhaps Rita would see how well I was doing and put me on the same level as the paperboy.

I waited outside the school. Suddenly the exits erupted with kids. I sat there sifting through the crowd of smiles and waves until I saw Rita, looking so happy, edge her way through the crowd. I noticed for the first time how terribly young she looked with her little knobby knees and youthful oily skin.

"Hi, June! You're back! You've been gone a whole year."

"Come on, hop in," I said. "I'll drive you home." I was trying to keep from sounding too eager.

"Oh, June, I can't. I'm meeting Jimmy. Haven't you heard? We're gonna be married after we finish school."

Hiding the hurt, I said, "No, I haven't heard, but I'm happy for you."

She gave a quick little wave with her fingers and said, "Gotta go. Call me sometime, June."

"Sure, sometime."

"Promise?"

"Sure," I said, forcing a smile.

"Gotta go. See ya. Gee, you're looking good."

As she waved and walked away, I knew I didn't belong there either, but where did I belong? I wanted to go home and talk to Mom, cry on her shoulder—not because of another rejection, but because of all the things going on in my life. Maybe she'd be there for me. But the house was full of visitors and my time at home had run out. I couldn't just spring something this important on them and leave. I'd have to find the right time. And I'd have to think of the right words. Mama knew I wasn't like other kids, but she still loved me. She would understand. After all, there were many other people like me, though sometimes it seemed most of them were hiding.

✳ ✳ ✳

My next booking was in Philadelphia. I left Pittsburgh and stopped in Greensburg to see Grandma. As I approached her porch I noticed three small flags from World War I in the front window. She was proud to have raised three sons who had fought for our country.

Since my grandmother didn't have a phone, my visit that day was a surprise. I caught her in a worried state. She was sad and concerned over the welfare of her cousin in Germany. She patted my hand as she said, "Oh, Chunie, you tank Got effer day dat you are free."

"I do, Grandma. I'm grateful," I said, and though I was sincere, I knew my gratitude was unequal to hers and would remain unequal until I had lived without freedom as she had.

With a road map beside me, I left for my next engagement at the Embassy Club in Philadelphia. While at home, I had been aware of the sugar, meat, and coffee shortages being a minor annoyance for Mom and Grandma. Also impossible to find were facial tissues for removing makeup, unless you knew someone, so everyone used a makeup towel. The towels were used and washed and used again. Women painted their legs with leg makeup instead of wearing hosiery because nylon was needed to make parachutes and military clothes. And for me, on the road, the gasoline situation became a critical issue. The gas stamps allotted weren't sufficient for traveling between cities from one booking to another. In fact, the average citizen was allotted only three gallons a week. So I inquired around the clubs I played, and I'd often find someone with extra stamps. Parking lot attendants and doormen usually had stamps on hand that they would sell for a dollar each. By asking around, I received enough stamps for five gallons a day. The price of gas stamps varied according to the size of the town; the ones in New York should have been delivered by limo, in boxes from Tiffany's.

Even with the help of club and hotel acquaintances and the availability of black market coupons, accepting a singing contract depended on my finding enough coupons to get there. Engagements weren't hard to come by, but it sometimes seemed as though gas coupons were controlling my career. At every turn, however, I saw servicemen and women who were ready to fight so we could all remain free. Rationing was a small price to pay.

Once the time wasted on buses and trains was eliminated, I had more time alone. I was working two weeks in each town, and soon I learned that life on the entertainment circuit wasn't all glamour, nor was it all work. Between rehearsals and traveling, a sense of humor was a prerequisite for survival.

During a long club engagement and extra USO and hospital

shows, I found that the daytime could drag. For someone who was trained to get up early, my days soon became boring. I knew no one since I was a single act, and besides, most show people sleep until it's time to go to work. In a new town I'd cover all the local shops, museums, daytime sporting events, and so on. Eventually, though, I'd run out of things to do.

Visiting local animal shelters helped relieve some of the loneliness, and there was one in every town. At that time you could adopt a pet for a small fee without additional contingencies. I would walk from one cage to another, wanting to take all the animals home. Finally, at one shelter, I picked out a pup, paid the $2, put him in the car, and vowed to find him a good home.

Back at the hotel, I bathed and groomed the small dog and named him Lucky. With the pup sporting a new collar, we went for a walk down to the lobby. Lucky turned out to be quite well mannered, a real charmer. The chambermaid fell in love with him and wanted one like him for her 10-year-old son. After learning more about her child, I felt he would be a good master for the dog, and Lucky was given a new home.

This experience showed me a way to save a few pets that otherwise might have been put to sleep. I decided to do this in every town I sang in whenever I had free time. That way I could help find homes for hundreds of animals. It amazed me to see how many animal lovers there were—doormen, desk clerks, waiters, hatcheck girls, bellboys, kitchen helpers; they were everywhere. Matching people with animals proved to be a rewarding activity, and I enjoyed being able to save the lives of so many animals.

Performing at night and running my informal pet adoption service in the daytime filled my hours pleasantly. One day, though, I came upon a beautiful white cocker spaniel puppy I couldn't give up. I named her Pam. It was much more fun to travel with her perched in the passenger's seat, and it was the best cure for loneliness on the road. Pam and

I were destined to spend years together. We traveled thousands of miles sharing good times and love. I took her to Bloomingdale's in New York and bought her everything they had for a dog her size. I dressed her in boots and coats and sleepers with bows around her ankles. She had a sailor outfit, a slicker for wet weather, and a bonnet and sunglasses for bright days. As we were driving along, heads would turn to look at Pam with her curls and bows flying out from under her sailor hat. She was a dear little pal, and being responsible for her made me feel more mature.

I was almost 18, and my career was rolling along smoothly. The reviews in *Billboard* and *Variety* were complimentary, but to me they sounded as though they were describing someone else. In one column, "Knight's Night Club Review," Gene Knight raved:

> If you want to see a dream walking, and singing as well, grab a chariot and whip over to the Harlequin where a flame-haired honey named June Walls is featured in a lively and colorful new show. Fresh from Hollywood, June brings an exceptionally good voice to the local cabaret scene and plenty besides...but plenty. When she sings "Chloe," you really go through smoke and flame.

These kinds of reviews not only helped boost my salary, but also brought offers for more appearances, and I began working with some of the finest people in the business: Carmen Cavallero, Phil Brito, Benny Goodman, Dennis James, Glenn Miller—all the great ones.

Not everyone liked my performances, but I never encountered a heckler I couldn't handle, because I was accustomed to ad-libbing between songs. On one occasion I was booked into a small club in Erie, Pa. For most of the engagement I'd been doing well, entertaining packed houses. But that

Saturday night I was in the middle of "Lady of Spain" when I heard a gruesome sound coming from the audience. In the darkness of the room I saw this figure of a man, roaming through the audience, gyrating and groaning to the music as I finished the song. Realizing his rudeness, the audience was 100% on my side. The man continued until I finished. The applause was thunderous, and as I bowed to the erupting sound, the man made his way onto the opposite side of the stage. He was trying to be funny, so I just stood there, still holding the mike, and watched. After a few minutes he returned to his seat as I quipped, "Isn't it amazing the kind of talent you get when you don't have to pay for it?" And the audience's applause finished him off. Still, the heckler, Don Rickles, sure went a long way from that small club in Erie.

While I was working in New York, a couple of USO Scouts came backstage to invite me to join an entertainment unit that was going overseas on February 22, 1943—the following year. I would be 18 in December '42 and would be of age. In order to get my papers processed for travel into a foreign country, though, the USO needed my parents' signature right away.

I crossed my fingers and said a prayer as I made the call. "Mom, it's a way for me to do my part," I said.

"No, June, I won't sign," she told me. "You do your part over here."

I heard Dad in the background saying, "What's wrong, Enzie? Is she OK?"

"But Mom," I argued, "the performers going are some of the best. There's a husband and wife comedy dance team, Lorraine and Roy Rognan, and Gypsy Markoff, and Jane Froman."

I heard her say, "Glenn, she's OK."

"Mom, I'd feel so privileged to be working with all of them. There's Grace Drysdale, a puppeteer and musician. There's another singer named Yvette."

"No, June, I won't sign it." That was final.

I was shocked to hear her sound so vehement, but I couldn't

change her mind, so I worked extra shows in hospitals and service clubs.

After my contract in New York ended, I was booked as the feature act at the Embassy Club in Philadelphia for two months. While there, toward the end of the contract, a 17-year-old singer from Huntington, WV, was on the bill with me. Her name was Phyllis Maelard, and this was one of her first engagements.

She wore no makeup, and she was a little awkward onstage, but she was beautiful. Her hair and eyes were deep brown, and her figure was like that of a swimwear model. After watching her show, I could see she was insecure about her performance.

The manager, Mr. Spatola, had Phyllis under contract, and one night he approached me. Combing his thinning hair with his fingers, he asked, "June, this…ah…Phyllis…she seems to have a lot of…ah…you know…could you give her a few pointers?"

Feeling like a real trouper, I said I'd see what I could do. Of course, I'd only been on the road a year myself. But you learn fast in show business.

Backstage between shows I spotted Phyllis sitting in her dressing room with her feet resting comfortably on a table. Peering around the door frame, I said, "Hi, I'm June."

"Come on in," she answered, standing and offering me a chair. "This is my first professional job, but I guess you could tell that, huh?"

She sat with one hip on a table, and with a shrug of defeat she added, "Oh, I've sung at service clubs a couple of times, and I did a show at Fort Pitt, but you're really good."

"Well, thanks." Spotting an opening for some constructive criticism, I said, "If you need any help, I'll be glad to…you know…"

Jumping to her feet, she said, "Would ya help me with my makeup? I've never worn it in my life. And my name—I hate my name."

We started working on her stage makeup, and soon she

was absolutely gorgeous. She had a sultry beauty, a look that didn't mesh with a name like Phyllis Maelard.

After recalling names of family and friends, she happened to mention that she was from Mingo County in West Virginia.

"Mingo! That's a good name," I offered.

"Mingo Maelard?" She looked incredulous, then smiled.

"No, wait, *Maynard*," I said. "That's better. Mingo Maynard."

"That's great!"

Thus Mingo Maynard was born.

We worked on her hair and then started on her song delivery. She caught on quickly. Onstage in full makeup, she could have been a stand-in for Ava Gardner. That night I watched her from the wings with Mr. Spatola, who was pleased.

"She sure is a knockout," he remarked. "You'll be pretty envious soon, huh?"

Mingo was stunning, but me envious? Never. To feel envious I would have had to feel like a woman, which I didn't. I could admire another woman's beautiful body but never my own.

Mingo and I were together constantly. I was proud of her progress, but with all the time we spent together, I was starting to have romantic feelings for her. In time, it was obvious that she cared for me, but since she was almost a year younger, a sexual unity had to be her decision. As the weeks passed, though, she expressed her feelings for me, and we began a wonderful romantic relationship.

My agent in Atlanta lined up an itinerary from Key West to Providence, R.I. During those months, Mingo traveled with me and watched my show nightly, learning all the while. My daily lessons were preparing her to be her best.

Several acts were on the bill with me at the club in Providence, including a comedian and a dance troupe called The Lola and Andre Dancers. Lola was a terrific performer— feminine, sensual, and gorgeous.

My contract at the club was for three months, at $200 a week, which was good money. At that time the average take-home pay was about $35 for a 40-hour week. With a long engagement such as this, I wanted to get an apartment with Mingo and live as other couples did. Mingo had no bookings for that period, so we agreed that my salary could support both of us.

After finding the perfect furnished apartment, I purchased all the necessities: sheets, pillows, tableware, towels, pots, and pans. We moved in and loved it. I was actually taking care of someone, and supporting her felt wonderful.

Then one rainy night, seven weeks into our blissful life, I came home to find a very solemn Mingo. "I've got to talk to you," she said. My first thought was that she was unhappy because she wasn't working. She practiced daily, but I knew she missed performing.

"Whatever it is, we can handle it, Mingo. What's wrong?"

"I can't be with you anymore."

"Look, we can handle whatever the problem is," I said. "We'll have your agent book you somewhere near where I'm working, and—"

"No! It's not that! June, I just can't be with you anymore," she said as she picked up her jacket and ran from the apartment.

She can't mean it, I thought. "Mingo, wait," I called out, then grabbed my coat and dashed after her. Breathless, I finally caught up to her at the corner under a streetlight. Turning her around, I looked into eyes of total sorrow. Tears flowed down her cheeks, which were wet with rain. Her sobbing was tearing me apart. I begged her to tell me what was wrong.

"I told you, I can't be with you anymore, June."

"What have I done?" I pleaded. "For God's sake, what have I done?" Whatever it was, it had to be a mistake, a misunderstanding. "Please tell me what it is. I know I can make it right."

"It's nothing you've done. It's just that you're you and I'm me and we simply don't go together."

I was so confused. "I think we go together very well."

"No," she said, "I'm just like you, just like you. Don't you know what I mean? I feel like you, think like you. We don't go together, that's all. We're not matched up right."

"Matched up? We're matched up perfectly."

"No, we're not. You know Lola from the dance troupe? She's truly feminine, she's beautiful. Well, that's the type of woman I want to be with. And you, you're...well, you're too masculine for me. You're not like Lola."

I had to lock my knees to keep from falling. "Mingo, what on earth are you saying?" I felt the pressure building in my head. I knew what she was saying.

I looked down at the water running from my trench coat, and it seemed like yesterday when I'd heard Rita say, "But why would I want you?" I wasn't what Rita wanted because I was a girl. Now I wasn't enough of a girl. Confused and depressed, I didn't know how to hit the happy medium or even locate it. *If they don't like girls, they don't like me*, I thought. *And if they do like girls, they don't like me. Where on earth do I belong?* Standing there, aware of the rain joining the tears on my face, I felt my heart breaking. I had so much to give but no one to give it to.

"June, the way you make love to me is the way I want to make love to a woman," Mingo said.

My heart sank.

"Would you want me to make love to you like that?"

"No," I answered sadly.

I finally understood. Whenever we made love, I was the dominant one. Evidently Mingo was butch, and I'd figured she was just passive. Then I recalled the words of Lee in Chicago: "Opposites attract."

"What are we going to do, Mingo?"

"I'm leaving for West Virginia in the morning."

I thought about the apartment, the tableware, the pots and pans, and the little girl I'd locked in the playhouse. Grandma's voice came to me clearly over the sound of rain: *If they don't want to be with you, a lock won't keep them.*

Reluctantly, the next day I drove Mingo to the bus station, knowing less about my life than ever. Where did I fit in? Of all the women I had met, none of them seemed right for me. I was becoming more and more disillusioned and was running short of options.

* * *

After completing an engagement in Key West, I was between club dates and had planned on spending a two-week vacation in Miami. The day before I was going to leave town, I approached a flight of stairs leading up to a restaurant. As I started up, my eyes followed each step before me until I saw, coming down the stairs, a pair of pink ankle-strapped shoes on the most beautiful pair of legs—all on a woman who stopped me cold.

Leaning against the railing and stepping back down, I gave her full access. She was a knockout in a pink halter sundress, and by the time she reached where I stood, I felt alive—for the first time in months, I felt truly alive.

Embarrassed over my actions, she merely smiled, lowered her dark eyes, and turned away. I stood mesmerized as I watched her smooth, sensual gait. I had to find out where she worked and arrange for an introduction.

At the club that afternoon, while looking for a piece of music I had misplaced, I saw her again. Key West is small, and as fate would have it, she was a featured dancer in the chorus line on an upcoming show.

After I had gathered my music, I sat at the horseshoe-shaped bar and ordered a drink. Many times an act that had closed would stay to watch the next show coming in. I just used that as a pretense, however, to observe this mystery woman. As I watched her rehearse, she seemed kind but cool, not the easiest person to get to know, so I asked the manager to introduce me when the woman took a break.

Her name was Diana Parker, and she told me she was from

Louisville, Ky., which became the topic of our first chat. While comparing club dates, we discovered that her opening show had been following my closing show in several towns.

Diana sat with me and talked between rehearsing her routines. She was a talented dancer and had previously performed with June Taylor. By the time the rehearsal ended, I had decided to stay in town one more night. My next club date was two weeks away, at the Five O'Clock Club in Miami.

My one-night stay-over turned into two, then three. Diana and I were having such fun and becoming fast and furious friends. She was both lovely in appearance and a beautiful person to know. She loved animals, music, art, and her country. Her dad was an NCO in the Navy, and her mother managed a Western Union office. She was an only child.

We laughed together and grew closer each day, so I extended my stay in Key West to two weeks so we could become better acquainted. There were night lunches, visits to other nightclubs, and long, barefoot walks on the beach. Diana glowed with a special kind of warmth when she looked at me, a look I'd never gotten from a woman before. But then perhaps she was looking deeper into my inner self than anyone else had. Perhaps she saw the depth of my contentment each time I looked at her.

One evening while we were walking along the beach, I felt the urge to explain my life to her, but I found myself stammering and pausing to find the right words. "And you know, Diana, when two people care for each other, well, it doesn't matter what kind of...uh..."

"June," she interrupted, looking at me, "what are you trying to say? That you're a homosexual?"

"Well, yes, but please don't let that scare you away."

She turned toward me and said, "Scare me away? Don't be silly. I kinda thought so."

"You did? Really?" I released a deep breath.

"Certainly," she said.

"That's OK?" I asked. And I saw her nod. Taking her in

my arms, I held her tightly. Moonlight shone on her hair, turning it into glowing, lustrous strands, and I thought, *I've finally found you.*

After that, Diana and I were together every minute, and a passionate romantic relationship quickly developed between us. We swam, shopped, saw the sights—you name it, we did it. I had a devoted affection for her and a craving to always be with her. I wanted to caress her, take pleasure and delight in her company, and protect her from harm forever. She made me slowly and gently take my time, as though we had a lifetime to consummate our love. At the beach the seagulls seemed to soar more gracefully, and the ocean rushing on the sand was like music to us. Together we felt a strange mystic quiet that made the rest of the world vanish.

By the time Diana's nightclub engagement had ended, we were totally fascinated with each other. I had found a deep friendship and a warm love for the first time, and a gauge by which I would, forever after, judge all other women.

Now I understood why my relationship with Mingo never would have worked. Diana was totally feminine. Mingo, like me, was very masculine. Once I realized this, Mingo and I became close friends.

As the months passed, my relationship with Diana continued. We corresponded every other day, either by mail or phone, and managed an evening together whenever our work would allow it. Pittsburgh was still my home base, where she could send mail and feel confident that I'd receive it. On my next trip home I was happy to find several letters from Diana.

My mother came into my room drying her hands on her apron. "You're reading your mail, huh?"

"I'll be finished in a minute," I told her.

"Who's this D. Parker, June?"

"A girlfriend."

"A girlfriend? Don't you have any boyfriends?"

"Well, Mom...I...look, I have to talk to you."

"June," she interrupted, "you're still a minor, and if I hear of any foolishness going on, you will not leave this house."

I felt myself swallowing the words. My mother stood in the doorway looking at me. She knew what I was going to say but didn't want to hear it.

It was just as well that my parents and I left the next morning for Greensburg. Visiting Grandma never ceased to educate me and effect a turn in my life.

On that visit I learned that shortly after my grandfather had died, Grandma had taken all her savings, $150, and made a down payment on a small house, which she cleaned, repaired, and painted, then offered for rent. As she explained to me, "Den I vould start all ofer, savink my money to buy anudder house to rent out." That's when she asked me to take her to the bank to buy her fourth house!

As we passed servicemen and women on the street, Grandma said, "In Churmany, day haf to get off de sidevalks and valk in de street, Chunie. My cousin says if day don't, de gestapo soldiers pushes dem off."

Grandma found a piece of tin as we walked. She picked it up and put it in her pocket to add to the tin cans she was saving for the scrap-metal drive. She also saved her pan drippings and meat fat for the war effort. They were needed to make soap, and she, like all of us, wanted to do her part.

Greensburg was still a small country town. Not much had changed in 13 years, except me. I felt considerably taller and a little worldlier as I held Grandma's hand and crossed the street to the small bank. She barely came to my shoulder as she shuffled along beside me, taking quick little steps, with her shoes on the wrong feet.

The nameplate on the desk read PRESIDENT. Of course, the bank was so small there were probably only four employees, including the president and the janitor.

Mr. Chapman, the 40ish dark-haired man seated at the desk, nodded to Grandma. "Mrs. Herman, what can we do for you?"

Grandma told him about the piece of property she wanted to buy. "I need $250 for de down payment, und I vill pay it back in a couple of veeks when I get de checks from de rentals on de first of de munt. I haf my money here in your bank." Shaking her arthritic finger at the bank president, she added, "Now, I don vont to pay intrust."

"Yes, Mrs. Herman," he smiled, "I know. We'll draw up the papers."

Mr. Chapman returned promptly with a paper for her to sign. She squinted at the document as she took her gold-rimmed specs from a hanky pocket, picked up the pen with her little wrinkled fingers, and signed the agreement. She received her loan without interest by using her own money as collateral, thereby freezing the interest payment on her savings until she repaid the loan.

As Mr. Chapman handed Grandma the check, her eyes revealed a smug little twinkle. She accepted it, turned to me, and said, "Come on, Chunie. Now ve go buy a piece of property." Although she was in her 90s, that day she was like a child full of love and excitement.

Grandma's example encouraged me even more to save my money until I had accumulated enough for a down payment on a house for Mom and Dad, who had never owned a home. Assuming that the high cost of medical bills, rent, food, clothing, and singing lessons had kept them from scraping together the down payment required, it seemed only right to begin paying them back.

My parents and I looked all over for a home that was both well built and inexpensive, until we found a two-bedroom stone house in Sheridan. It sat on the edge of a cliff and overlooked the Allegheny. The walls were 12 inches thick, and the house had been built by a stonemason who had carved funny little faces in the chimney. It also had a fenced-in yard and a large porch that Mama loved. From the porch you could watch the barges going up and down the river. It was an old house with no insulation, but for the price we were paying, we couldn't expect Shangri La. And anyway, Mama loved it. The price was right, and I had the 10% to put down.

"My goodness!" Dad exclaimed. "A home of our own!"

"Our very own home," Mom added. "I can't believe it. Oh, Junie, thank you, thank you."

Mom and Dad hugged me tightly. Nothing I'd ever done before had made anyone so happy. I felt proud giving them something they'd never had.

Together we worked to whip the house into shape. And I remember the lonely-sounding horns from the barges in the night as they slipped by. The beams of their spotlights, searching from left to right, cut huge white streaks in the fog. How secure I felt listening to the ships' *WHOOoooo, WHOOooooo,* knowing the house we were in was ours and I was singing for it. That was 1942, and I was just 17.

The house was a small part of the promise that began in Mrs. Bickel's living room. She had soft, upholstered chairs and a chandelier with many lights, while we had straight-back chairs and our chandelier was a lightbulb hanging from the center of the ceiling. Sitting in Mrs. Bickel's living room while she ran for her 11 cents to pay me for bread, I had promised myself, *Someday I'll get nice things like this for Mama.* But this was only the beginning. There would be another house, a better one, and they could both quit working. I would make sure of that.

$$* \quad * \quad *$$

In December, when I turned 18, I went home for my birthday. Mom handed me a stack of mail, including many letters from Diana. Happiness was written all over my face. I'm certain Mom noticed and was once again curious about this "D. Parker" who had been writing since I'd left home.

Diana and I had been together several times that year, and our relationship was growing more serious. I took her letters to my room to read privately and was halfway through the last one when my mother knocked on the door.

"Can you come out here, June? I want to talk to you. Come to the kitchen and tell me what you've been doing lately."

I had anticipated the interruption but hoped it wouldn't happen until I had rested, especially since I'd driven 15 hours straight from Florida. With two weeks until my next club date, I had ample time to talk to her, but she called, so I quickly folded the last letter, closed my bedroom door behind me, and walked into the kitchen.

This would be the time to tell them, I thought. I felt strong, and in my heart I knew I was right; my feelings were genuine.

In the hallway I passed the many photographs Mom had framed, and I thought, *Even if they don't understand, I'll still have their love. I'm sure of that.*

I was sitting at the table answering Mom's usual questions about the places I'd worked, the dangers of traveling alone, and the friends I had met. When she asked another usual question—"Have you met anyone you're interested in?"—I took the opportunity to say, "Yes, and I want to talk to you about it."

"Oh!" she replied. "Who is he?"

"That's what I want to talk to you about," I continued softly. "It's not a he, it's a she."

My mother had been standing at the kitchen sink piddling around with food for supper, and as though she had been waiting for me to drop the bomb, she had her response ready. She whipped around, threw a knife in the sink, and yelled, "I will have no daughter of mine like that. I always knew you were different!" Then the yelling turned to high-pitched screaming. "Who did this dirty thing to you?" she said, slamming the cabinet drawers.

"Nobody did anything to me," I said calmly. "I've always felt this way, but I never understood why before."

"It's sick, sick, sick, and you'll go straight to hell. The Bible says it's wrong. Didn't you learn anything at Bible school?"

"I learned to tell the truth, and I'm telling it. This isn't something I decided to experiment with."

"It's dirty, it's wrong, it's a sin!" she shouted. "Why can't you be normal and find a man? Huh? Why?"

"Because the way I feel, that would be wrong."

"Well," she said, slamming more cabinet doors and drawers, "tell me, just what do you do in bed with a woman?"

"Please, Mom! Get your mind above my belt!"

"Do you have any idea how this makes me feel?" she asked, but before I could answer, she added, "It makes me wish you were dead."

"Mom! How can you say that?" I couldn't believe my own mother could say something so malicious to me, her only daughter. "Please understand how this makes me feel" were the last words I said before she raised her hand and gave me a staggering blow across the face. As much as it hurt physically, it couldn't compare to the wound she had driven inside, which jarred my very soul. She had never hit me before. She had been so proud while I was working with her or singing. For the first time, I realized she was only interested in what I could do for her. I was torn apart and couldn't hold back the tears.

Dad came into the kitchen anxiously asking, "What's wrong?"

My mother screamed the news to him, "She's sleeping with women, that's what's wrong!" Dad straightened his back, pulled in his chin, and cleared his throat as Mom continued, "And we can all thank your side of the family for this."

Dad snapped back, "Now, you keep my family out of this." Then Mom directed her wrath at me again. My father was far calmer than I, perhaps because one of us had to be.

Through my tears, I tried to explain my feelings and thoughts, hoping she would understand, but nothing worked; in fact, things just got worse.

"Would you have wanted me to lie to you?" I asked. "If

I can't come to you with the truth, where can I go?"

She turned toward me with a look of bitter hatred. I had never before seen so much animosity in one face. "I'll tell you where you can go," she screamed. "You can get out. Get out of this house and don't ever come back!"

Storming through every room, she grabbed photos of me from the mantle and walls and smashed them to the floor. Scrapbooks, snapshots, anything she saw ended up in the garbage. Her sudden outburst sent a paralyzing shock through me. I remained numb as she continued, "I'd rather see you dead than living with a woman!"

Hearing that and seeing her abomination completely tore me apart. There was no reality, no future or past, only the outside layer of me. It was the beginning of the loneliest part of my life. I had crossed many obstacles in my 18 years, but I knew this was more than I could cope with.

I went to my room and started packing. How could she turn on me so bitterly? I hadn't changed. Now that she had learned the truth, I was an outcast.

As I threw the last of my luggage into the car, Dad came running toward me. "She'll get over it," he said, trying to console me. "You know, honey, she's right about my side of the family. My brother's son William and my sister Pearl are just like you. Give your mother time."

I was too stunned to reply. Dad's arms were around me, and I saw him open the car door, but I was still in shock. I must have started the car and pulled away from the curb, but was unaware of doing so. With the highway before me, I drove trying to see the road through tear-filled eyes, not knowing where to go. My next club date was two weeks away. Mile after miserable mile I drove. Several times I had to pull off the road to let the tears fall freely. I thought about my Aunt Pearl, who had died when I was young, and my cousin William, who was an army pilot. I had never known they were gay. But if Mom knew about them, why couldn't she accept me? Everything I had ever done was for her. Now my whole world had collapsed. I felt I would never get over witnessing her wrath or losing her acceptance. Obviously all she ever wanted was to have me achieve, to attain success. Success, always success—that would get her. I'll succeed, I thought. Then she could put the pictures back on the mantel and brag to her friends.

Without my knowledge, my mother was planning her own strategy. The following day she phoned Diana's mother and advised her to confiscate my letters in order to stop our relationship.

Four

Broadway and Beyond

From that day on, determination fueled me As if I were running on hot coals, from my first waking moment until my last, I pushed myself to succeed for my mother. I drove from Pittsburgh to New York and to Key West and back, with contracts to sing in every city along the way. In Atlanta I bought a house, just to have a place to call home.

For months my work seemed to be getting better. Then, on February 23, 1943, I read the horrible news story that an airplane, a Yankee clipper, had crashed over Lisbon, Portugal. It was the USO Unit I had wanted to join and the one for which Mama had refused to sign.

Two of the seven entertainers were killed: a Russian singer named Tamara (the woman who had taken my place when my mother had refused to let me join), and Roy Rognan, the male partner in the dance team. Jane Froman, Gypsy Markoff, Grace Drysdale, Lorraine Rognan, and Yvette all suffered injuries, from severe to minor. It was horrifying to know that I should have been on that flight, but I found comfort in the thought that somewhere someone was watching over me.

During that time, though, I was extremely lonely, but I was

thankful for my little dog. She accepted me when my mother and society hadn't. Pammie knew no prejudice. She always remained in the dressing room while I was onstage. After each show, she would be quietly waiting for me. Every night I thanked God for little Pam.

One night while performing at an enlisted men's club at Fort Pitt, I was singing a requested ballad, "This Is My First Affair, So Please Be Kind." Someone accidentally opened the dressing-room door, and Pammie ran onstage, her tail wagging so hard the curl at the end was a blur. Still singing, I scooped her up and placed her on top of the piano. She had charm, not to mention audience appeal. As I sang to her, she listened intently and turned her head from side to side. She enjoyed being with me, and the servicemen and women were so delighted with her that from then on she appeared at the end of my act. On cue, a busboy let her loose and she bounded onstage. I had a song written for her called "I Like You." Together we sat on top of the piano as I sang: "I like you / I like you a whole lot / I like you for being all the things I'm not..." Within the 32 bars of music were lyrics that were perfect to be sung to a little puppy, and often we received a standing ovation.

Pammie and I continued to be booked into many interesting clubs. We traveled to Boston, where I worked eight weeks at the Satire Room, and then back to one of my favorites, Philadelphia's Embassy Club, where my contract lasted several months.

Settling in Philadelphia for a long period of time enabled me to try to get in touch with Diana in Louisville. If by chance I could catch her at home between bookings, she could come meet me. Directory assistance gave me her parents' number, and as luck would have it, she answered the phone.

"Diana! This is June!"

She said she was pleasantly surprised, and we spoke for a minute, but she sounded strange.

"What's wrong, why are you whispering?"

"I can't talk now—Mother's home. I'd love to see you. I've

got to talk to you." She had two weeks off between club dates, so I suggested she fly to Philly.

"Yes," she whispered, "I'll get the first flight in the morning and call you from the airport."

"I'll be at the hotel," I said, then heard her hang up.

The hours dragged, but Diana finally arrived, looking happy to see me. My excitement soared as I ran to greet her. We talked as we walked to my car. Once inside, she turned toward me, and I saw tears on her lovely face.

"Your mother called my mom. She has your letters. I can't see you anymore."

"Then how did you get away?"

"After I got off the phone with you, I told Mom it was a call from my agent. She thinks I'm working. The pressure from her is agonizing. Each trip home it's the same thing: 'When are you going to get married?' It's depressing. I dread going home. After your mom called, Mother said, 'What would people say if they found out?' I said, 'Damn people. It's my life!'"

After having been through the ordeal with my own mother, I felt as though I was reliving the hell of it all over again. "You have to be honest," I said. "Stand up for yourself."

She covered her face with her hands and cried, "I can't. It's hell at home."

I wanted so much to take on her problems, but then I realized that *I* was her problem.

"Please listen, please stop crying," I said. "I can fix this. I won't write you anymore. I can see this is too much for you, and you can't spend your life on the road simply because you dread going home. So write me through my agent if you want, but if you decide not to, I'll understand."

Our three days and nights together ended sadly. More than anything I wanted to be with her. When we were together I felt a radiant glow surrounding us. The rest of the world just happened to be there. The pain was unmerciful when we parted, but Diana had to leave for Louisville and get back to reality.

I had to go on with my life too. But during each performance, I relived the tenderness of the last three days. It became
easier for me to understand the meaning of the lyrics, and
every phrase was pulled from my soul to give forth the love I
felt for her. It was another facet of my learning, and in some
ways it hardened me.

One night at the Embassy Club, Georgie, the maid who
looked after my wardrobe, entered my dressing room bursting
with excitement. "Isn't it wonderful, Miss June? Isn't it just
wonderful?"

"Isn't what wonderful?"

"Haven't they told you? Didn't you see today's
Philadelphia Enquirer?"

"Oh, Georgie, I haven't had time to read a paper!" I
laughed. She turned quickly, and after some scurrying around
and mumbling, I heard, "Just you wait. Just wait till you see."
She found a copy, came rushing to me, then reached out and
hugged me as I read:

> The Mighty Mite (as Broadway knows is
> Billy Rose) wants June Walls, the startlingly
> beautiful redhead of the Satire Room, to call
> him at once and arrange an audition. The MM
> is casting his new musical *The Seven Lively
> Arts*.... Producer Rose was impressed by the
> 'rave' staged by a Boston newspaperman in
> Miss Walls' behalf. And singing leading ladies
> with looks are scarce!

Georgie and I spun around and jumped with joy. I grabbed
my little dog and held her high in the air. "We're on our way,
Pammie! Billy Rose wants us to call!"

I phoned that night and made an appointment for the
following afternoon.

As I drove to New York City, I felt confident despite my
anxiety. That afternoon I met with Mr. Rose. "You've got a

powerful voice, June," he said. "They heard you in front of the theater, with no mike. That's great!"

Mr. Rose wanted me for the part, and I apprised him of my contract with the Embassy Club. He asked if it would be a hardship to commute to New York every day for rehearsals until my Embassy contract ran out. *Hardship?* I thought. *How many years has it taken me and my family to make this dream come true?* I assured him that I could sing nightly in Philly and drive to New York daily. I made plans to finish my contract, give up my option for a longer contract, and move to New York.

Rehearsals commenced immediately and continued every afternoon, five days a week. During one rehearsal, Mr. Rose asked me to run through a new song, "Every Time We Say Goodbye." I joined a rather small older man on the piano bench as he shifted the melody to my key. He seemed to have a special fondness for the song, and we sang it together several times. He was helpful, and I thanked him for handling the introduction so gently. Later I understood why the song was so important to him: He had written it. He was Cole Porter!

It was a thrill working with such famous people, and I couldn't help thinking of Mom. *When she learns that I'm in a Broadway show and the whole world is opening up for me, things will be better between us,* I thought. And I wanted so much to write to Diana, to tell her the good news, but my letters would only cause trouble for her at home. It made me realize I had no one with whom to share my good fortune.

My last night at the Embassy was sad. Everyone was happy for me, but it was like saying goodbye to my family. The club had been my home for months.

Early the next morning I packed the convertible, checked out of the Walton Hotel with Pam, and headed north. In New York City I drove from hotel to hotel for two and a half hours. With each stop I'd get the same answer: "Lady, don't you know there's a war on?"

I had to postpone my search since I was due at rehearsal. Pammie made the hotel situation more difficult, but it certainly couldn't be impossible. Surely someone with the show would know where to find a room, I thought, as I rushed through the theater entrance. They probably even had rooms set aside for emergencies such as this. I talked to a few people, and Mr. Rose learned of my predicament.

"Don't worry," he said. "After rehearsal we'll find you a place."

But when rehearsal ended he told me he hadn't had any luck either. After searching through his pockets, he said, "Here, take this," and handed me a key. "It's mine, but I won't be needing it."

"Are you sure? Won't it put you out?"

"It's no bother. We keep this room for times like this."

Mr. Rose reassured me, saying he would be going home, and I gratefully took the key, realizing I'd been right: They did have rooms set aside for emergencies.

The room turned out to be a gorgeous, elegant suite at the Astor Hotel. With gratitude and humility, I thought, *Ordinary people with pups must stay at the Astor too!* A bellboy placed my luggage on a rack and opened the window to welcome in a cool New York breeze. Pammie and I were like two waifs in paradise. The tiled bathroom, with its metallic wallpaper and fancy fixtures, must have cost a bundle. I put the dog's food and water dishes on the bathroom floor, and we enjoyed the fineries that were new to both of us.

The next few days were terrific. I stayed busy learning my role, and Mr. Rose was pleased with my progress. Best of all, Cole Porter liked the way I sang his song.

Several nights later Pammie rose from the foot of the bed growling, softly at first then more loudly. I reached for her, but she was already headed for the door.

"Is anyone there?" I listened for a response and suddenly heard the metal cylinders click in the lock. A vertical strip of light cut through the darkness and slowly widened.

Backlighting from the hall revealed the silhouette of a man in a wide-brimmed hat and long overcoat.

"Mr. Rose!"

"I just came to pick up some things," he said calmly.

I was kneeling upright on the bed with the sheet pulled high under my chin. He opened several dresser drawers but disturbed nothing. Finally, he turned, threw his hat and coat on a chair, and walked toward me. The look on his face was terrifying, so I jumped from the bed in fear. Pammie's growl turned to a shrill bark.

My long-buried memory of that horrible night in the car engulfed me. But now I was older; I knew what he wanted. Only this time I was trapped. I needed a weapon but had nothing.

Mr. Rose grabbed at my pajama top. "My God! What are you doing?" I yelled. "Please! Please!" He pushed me against a wall and pressed his body into mine. Terror turned to fury, and I broke away, only to be caught again moments later. As he chased me through the rooms, Pammie barked and pulled at his pant legs. I dodged around furniture to keep distance between us, but I could get no more than an arm's length away. Mr. Rose grabbed me, ripping my pajama top. He knocked a chair aside, and I turned, running blindly into a wall. In confusion, I had trapped myself in a corner at the head of the bed.

He lunged, smiling a sickening grin, and caged me with his arms and body. With both hands gripping my waist, he lifted me and threw me onto the bed. The whipping motion forced my arms over my head, and instantly he was on me, wedging himself between my thighs. I felt his forearm across my shoulders and neck, pressing my back into the mattress. Looking over my shoulders, I tried to stretch my arms to reach the nightstand, a lamp, anything...I heard the sound of his zipper, and then he forced himself on me.

I lay rigid with disgust for several minutes as he violated my body. *Dear God, there has to be a way out of this.* My mind was racing. Then, like a deep whirling echo, I recalled his words—"You've got a powerful voice, June!"—and realized I had a weapon.

With my hands locked behind his neck, I pulled his head toward mine and yelled, "Get off me, you son of a bitch, or I'll bust your fuckin' eardrum!" Sucking in air to fill my lungs, I was ready to let go with crystal-shattering pitch and volume. I felt him cringe. He sank, exhaled the breath from his gut, and held it, as though contemplating something. His arm relaxed across my chest. I closed my eyes tightly as his body moved off mine, and once again I heard his zipper. Pulling the sheet over my torn pajama top, I sat trembling at the side of the bed, anticipating anything. He picked up his hat and coat and left, closing the door quietly. I was terrified that he'd come back. He could have. He had the key. I felt I had set myself up for this—trusting, always trusting. I always saw the good in people.

I'll be crucified if people find out what happened, I thought, *and violated if they don't.*

Pammie jumped on the bed and into my arms. I held her, and the two of us trembled. Afraid to sleep, I lay awake, frightened of what might happen. At last, I was thankful when morning came. I felt an oppressive heaviness in my throat and dreaded going to the theater.

As I'd expected, that day everything went wrong at rehearsal. The man who had been so pleased the day before hid in the darkness of the balcony shouting, "I can't hear you! You're not projecting. Try again!"

I started again, only to be interrupted by his bark. "You're not delivering up here. Take it from the top."

Over and over I'd begin, and he'd yell, "I can't hear you!"

Finally, Mr. Rose said, "That's it, Red. You're not producing. You're out of this show."

A sort of madness erupted inside me. "I don't deserve this!" I yelled. "My God, do I have to sleep with you to be in this show? Is that what I have to do to succeed? What about determination, talent, and hard work—don't they count?" I looked at the faces of each of the cast members and stage-hands, and I looked at Cole Porter and felt humiliated. "No! I don't have to do that! I'm not wrong!" Then I felt the same unrestrained anger that had burst forth the night before.

I walked to center stage, reached for the mike, and addressed the hidden figure in the balcony. "Mr. Rose, how's this for projecting?" Speaking as clearly as past training prompted, I continued, "The voice hasn't changed. It's the same one you've admired for weeks. But while the rest of the cast was sleeping last night, you were chasing me around your suite at the Astor Hotel. You failed, so I'm fired! And it's not because I haven't produced today. It's because I didn't produce *last night*. But if this is the criteria for being in a Billy Rose show, I hope you rot in hell with it!"

The rest of the cast turned away, not wanting to jeopardize their jobs. Out of view of the balcony, however, I heard and saw many affirmative remarks and looks—perhaps from women who at one time had had to succumb to the Mighty Mite.

My dreams of being in a Broadway show were destroyed, but I left with my pride and decency intact—even though the hard fall had knocked the wind out of me. Still, I was learning the game. The people around me were teaching me well. The object was to trust none of them until they proved themselves, and then always be on guard. My innocent thoughts were gone; I was standing against everyone else, alone.

After packing everything I owned into the car, I stashed all my money—$175—into my makeup kit, and Pam and I left the Astor. I started making the rounds of hotels again, hoping to quickly find a room so I could meet with agents and line up work.

Pammie waited patiently in the car while I dashed in and out of hotel lobbies. All evening I drove from one hotel to another. Signs across town read NO VACANCY since servicemen had well-deserved priority. I grew tired and was feeling more depressed each time I left the comfort and lights of a hotel lobby. I was ready to give up when I approached the night clerk at the New Yorker Hotel. "A room?" he said. "Sure! Register right here."

Exhausted, I quickly filled out the card he pushed in front of me. At least tonight Pam and I could sleep safely in a room of our own. Bellboy trailing, I led the way to the car but stopped in horror at the curb. In the few minutes it had taken me to register, someone had slashed the convertible's top to pieces and stolen everything inside. I never carried a handbag, so every penny I had was in my makeup case, which I'd also left in the car. Pammie cowered in the backseat. The only other thing left in the car was her box of treats. I picked up my dog, hugged her, and carried her into the lobby.

The night manager alerted the police, and they made out a report. At last I was led to my room, with no luggage, nothing. Over three years I had carefully accumulated gowns, photographs, and musical arrangements, and now I only had the clothes on my back. What would I do? The thief had stolen more than my belongings, more than the tools of my trade. What little faith and trust I'd had left were gone as well.

The bellboy led me to my room, where he opened a window then handed me the key. He left, knowing I had no money to give him. The enormity of what had happened washed over me as I leaned against the door. Then suddenly I felt a wet stream running down my legs. I looked down to see a growing pool of blood at my feet. I was hemorrhaging! Blood flowed down my legs in gushes, filling my shoes.

Anger and disgust such as I had never known exploded. I pulled off my shoes and hurled them across the room through the open window, yelling, "Here, you bastard! Take these too! You've taken everything else!"

The rage wanted out. I felt the need to strike back and inflict some hurt of my own but couldn't release it. I ran to the window and looked down. Seventeen floors below the bloody shoes in the middle of the street were barely visible. No one even looked at them. No one gave a damn. They didn't even know I existed.

Rushing to the bathroom, I soaked a towel in cold water and began scrubbing the bloody carpet. I was enraged to think of all the things that had happened, which made the hurt from the loss of my mother and Diana cut even deeper.

The harder I scrubbed, the more I vowed "I will not submit and jeopardize my principles and morals." Rinsing the blood-soaked towels in the tub, I prayed, "Dear God, help me. If I'm wrong for standing up to them, please show me. But if I'm right, let me know that too." The red water ran from the towels as I continued to hemorrhage. Crying aloud, I prayed, "Please give me courage to face discrimination. With strength from you, I can do it. I *will* do it. They will accept me as I am. I'll make them accept me."

I had been trying to escape the barriers placed around me by society. Looking so feminine in the eyes of all those close to me felt crippling. I had lost my dear mother, the show, and the one person I deeply loved.

I reviewed my options. Calling home was out of the question; I would ask my mother for nothing. Although I still sent money home every week, my letters went unanswered. This hurt deeply and cemented her words: "I wish you were dead."

After the rug was cleaned and drying, I sat holding my little dog. She was all I had. And then I thought, *But I'm all she has too. I have to make it for her.*

A new determination was born that night, one so strong it made my earlier resolve look simple and childish. The songs and audience were still there. Better arrangements could be written. Better pictures and gowns and a more spectacular performance each time I walked onstage would make them know the real me, instead of all the glamour. By God, I vowed to have success.

Counting my blessings, I could still rely on a voice that had performed wonderfully so far, as well as Pammie's unquestioning devotion, my car, and my experiences over the past three years. Realizing I had to keep going, I picked up the phone and called AGVA, the American Guild of Variety

Artists. The call was turned over to Jackie Bright, who listened to my story and called it one of the worst strokes of luck he had ever heard. He promised to send one of the office personnel over to assist me in getting started again.

When the woman arrived, I felt like a drowning person who had been thrown a life preserver. She made notes as I told her about the stolen things and reeled off the basics I would need to get started. She left with quite a list.

When she returned, it was like Christmas, with all the packages she brought. She had coffee and sandwiches for the two of us, dog food for Pammie, and clothes for me—slacks, sneakers, and casual things. And I couldn't stop the tears of gratitude.

I returned to the AGVA office with her. The staff made phone calls on my behalf, and in minutes I was offered a contract in Boston. I had no gowns or music, but after I accepted the offer, AGVA advanced me $200 to cover my travel expenses and necessities. Never in my life had I been more grateful.

Thinking I had cleared the worst and nothing that terrible could happen again, I left for Boston knowing my dues were paid in full. The engagement was successful and others followed, as I slowly restored my music, wardrobe, and a fragile faith in humanity.

* * *

Broadway holds tough lessons for the countless hopefuls who innocently arrive with dreams of success. All too often most are doomed to disappointment. My toughest lesson was learning that no one really cared. Even Mom wouldn't answer my letters, so I began to feel that everyone was trying to weaken me, to see me crumble. Regardless of how well I did, the fear of another face leering from a darkened hallway lingered in my mind.

Life would have been easier if I'd been able to take it with less intensity, sensitivity, and vulnerability. But that same sensitivity was the key to performing, a link that kept me fine-tuned to the music and the audiences.

I tried to keep a positive outlook, but it was hard not to be depressed by the war. The front pages of local papers ran casualty lists of men and women who had been killed the previous day. One day I received a letter from Florence, one of the WACs I had met at the Bluegrass Room years before, who told me that our friend Robert, the army sergeant, had been killed in North Africa.

The headlines were frightening. Russia and Germany had invaded both Romania and Hungary. As I read news of the war in Europe, Hitler's forces seemed to grow stronger with each invasion, when in fact, as we learned later, the German army was spread out so thinly all over Europe that it weakened the units and deteriorated the morale of the men. The turning point, however, came on June 6, 1944, D-Day, when the Allies landed at Normandy. The loss of life was enormous, but it was the beginning of the end of the war in Europe.

Aware of the hell that so many men and women my age were going through, I had nothing to complain about. In fact, it made me want to work harder for them. I had always driven myself, but I was becoming a tougher taskmaster. Every day I phoned USO and U.S. service personnel in charge of entertainment. I searched for new and better agents, different music and more powerful arrangements, and more gorgeous gowns.

Returning to New York was my ultimate goal. At that time it was the only place in the country to land that big break. All the famous nightclubs were there, and if I wanted prestige, that's where I had to be. For that I needed a good agent or manager, so I asked around at the clubs and read *Billboard* to learn the names of the best agents. One mentioned repeatedly was Lou Perry at the Bryant Hotel.

A phone call secured an office meeting where Lou could hear me sing. He was handling two fellows at the time: Sonny King and Dean Martin. After watching me perform during a club date, he said I still had a lot to learn.

The style I had learned from Billie Holiday was best suited for smaller clubs. Lou wanted me to learn how to handle the large rooms and theaters, since that's where I could make the most money. He booked me just enough so I'd have money in my pocket but still have time to go to the Copacabana to study Jane Froman's style. And that's the way it all began.

Lou introduced me to Sonny and Dean, who were both singers and rather good-looking. Lou took us to the Havana Madrid, the Latin Quarter, and the Copacabana every night to learn our trade by watching other performers, and we became a regular foursome at those three clubs.

Dean was married and had a baby, and every penny he had went to his wife and child. I never knew where they stayed, but most of the time Dean slept in the lobby of the Bryant Hotel. He was skinny, always hungry, and I felt sorry for him. Every morning I'd stop by the hotel lobby, where he was usually curled up on a couch.

"Hi!" I'd say. "I'll buy breakfast."

Hearing that, he'd sit up, stretch, and in a second he'd be on his feet. "Mmm, boy!" he'd say, "I can smell that bacon aaaaall the way around the corner."

Every night we were back at the clubs to watch the shows. At the Havana Madrid, Lou would find an out-of-the-way spot where we could watch the show, and leave us there. But Dean wasn't about to be told what to do.

"You gonna be OK, June?" he'd ask.

"I'll be OK, Dean, but I'm not so sure about you." Then he'd start to circulate, chatting with the customers. After introducing himself to a couple, he'd take a cigarette from the gentleman's cigarette case, light it, then after a few minutes he'd take one of their drinks, propose a toast, and down the drink. He'd come back to Sonny and me, and say, "Did ya see that?"

"Yes, Dean! You're gonna make somebody mad."

But he never did. The customers went along with his actions as if they were part of the show. Everyone knew they weren't. But they loved it anyway.

We'd often witness Dean steal a show by singing along with a performer who was onstage. I told him he'd never amount to anything acting up that way. But when I'd lecture him, his hands would come up and he'd start singing, "Oh, I'm hittin' the trail...On the lone prairie..." And off he'd go. His voice was good, but above all he was an entertainer.

One night while a young comedian was performing, Dean walked onstage, moved in front of the act—a cardinal sin in show business—took over the mike, and started singing "San Fernando Valley." I thought the bouncers would kick him out, but they didn't. The comedian stayed cool throughout the interruption and broke up the audience with his antics in back of Dean. The comic, Jerry Lewis, was a natural, and his response only made him funnier. Afterward Dean and Jerry pooled their talents, with Lou managing them both.

In the meantime, Lou dropped me off each night at the Copa to watch Jane Froman. After a long recovery from a plane crash, which mangled both of her legs, she had returned to the stage more dynamic than ever.

"Study everything Jane Froman does," Lou advised. "She's the best. You can't do better than that."

The club, decorated with white palms, white leaves, and gold ornamentation, enhanced Jane's elegance as the emcee introduced her. The lights dimmed. Then came total blackness, intensified by a soft drum roll, which gradually built to a crescendo. Then silence...and then the sound of a lovely voice: *Someday he'll come along...* A downbeat came, hard and heavy. *...the man I love.* Another downbeat... *And he'll be big and strong...the man I love...*

A pinspot illuminated a beautiful woman seated atop a grand piano. And from that instant she owned the audience. No one moved, breathed, or existed in the circle of her spell.

Lou was right. She was the epitome of an entertainer. To captivate an audience like that, to make people forget everything, was awe-inspiring. I would do that someday. With Jane Froman's power and Billie Holiday's intimacy with an audience, I could have an act as strong as both of theirs.

✳ ✳ ✳

Dean and Jerry began occupying all of Lou's time and growing more sensational as they polished their act. Eventually, Lou had to drop Sonny and me, while Martin and Lewis went on to make entertainment history. I was happy for Dean, but now I had to find another Lou Perry.

Experimenting with my new delivery while singing at Bill Miller's Riviera, I started getting better reviews. There I met Bobby Cohen and his wife. Bobby co-owned the club and was also part owner of the Embassy Club in Manhattan. But his main business, he told me, was a hardware store in Trenton, NJ. Bobby was about 45 and slightly balding. Easy living had packed a few pounds onto his 5-foot-11 frame, but he was always well dressed and polite—a real gentleman. He knew nothing about show business but a lot about managing. At the end of the last show one night, I joined him at his table, and he began to discuss business.

"June," he said, "I'd like to manage your career and make things happen, but there's one drawback."

"What's that?"

"Let's say I manage to get you close to the top, and some joker comes along and you get married. Where does that leave me after I've worked to build you?"

I laughed, and he watched as a wide smile spread across my face. "It'll never happen, Bobby." Looking directly at him to catch his reaction, I said, "I like women."

Stunned, he remained quiet for a moment, then picked up his drink and jiggled the ice in his glass. Then I saw a twitching in the corner of his mouth that ended in a big grin.

"Terrrrific," he said, toasting me with his glass. "You'd

probably work like hell for a career." He nodded, confirming his own statement, and after a pause added, "But you know, it may be necessary to bend a little at some point. You know, to get that big break with the right person." I knew, but I could only stare at him in silence.

Hours later, after much deliberation, we both felt we had a mutual reason to enter into a contract together. Bobby had business connections with several clubs besides his own, which would keep me working and build my name. And in building me, he too would reap rewards.

Bobby hired two publicity men, Bill Fix and Syd Panzer. With their help, I was working continuously, and the money and publicity were growing.

Early one morning the phone rang. It was Bobby.

"Hi," he said. "Let's go shopping. You need some new gowns, and I've got three hours before my train leaves for Trenton. I'll pick you up in half an hour."

That sounded good to me since I'd never been a pro at choosing gowns. I got ready and scurried down to the lobby and out the door just as Bobby pulled up in a cab. He directed the driver to Madison Avenue, and we arrived at a shop with a red gown in the window.

"What do you think?" he said, pointing at it.

"That? You're kidding! I can't wear red!"

"Just try it, OK?"

The gown was fitted, a radiant Chinese red. Walking out of the dressing room in it, I ran both hands through my hair, fluffing out every red strand to prove my point. Bobby tossed his newspaper in the air, and I heard "Wow!" followed by "Looks like you were poured in and forgot to say 'when.'"

It made me laugh; he was typical. Poor guy—he'd have taken poison if it were offered in a diamond-studded vial.

"You like it, Bobby? Will this get 'em?"

"Yeah! That'll get 'em!" he said, mimicking my tone.

After choosing several more gowns, Bobby signaled for the

clerk to write up the purchases. When the clerk had gone, he opened a briefcase jammed with stacks of hundreds and slipped out the cash to pay for the gowns.

"Good Lord!" I said. "Where'd you get all that dough? There must be a million bucks in there!"

Bobby motioned for me to be quiet as I looked at him in disbelief.

We left the shop and hurried to a restaurant. Sipping coffee, I remained quiet, only staring at him.

"I know you want to know what I'm doing," Bobby finally said. "Well, I run money out of town. Some business-men can't trust their own people." He let out a chuckle and added, "I guess it takes a Jew boy to be trusted."

That was all the explanation I needed. Evidently he was laundering money, and I felt safer not knowing any more about the operation.

After a quick glance at his watch, Bobby downed his last swallow of coffee. "See you next week," he said with the usual tip of his hat, and off he went.

The following week I had many questions on my mind. Though I thought I knew Bobby, sometimes it was hard for me to figure him out. Whatever city I was working in, he would be there smiling and happy, with new contracts for engage-ments, always at excellent clubs. Gradually, though, I realized that the longer I knew him, the less I knew about him.

Still, we worked well together and had a wonderful rap-port that put us both at ease. Once, while we were having cocktails at El Morocco, I noticed a table of five or six men in expensive tailored suits mumbling among themselves but obviously looking toward our table. Bobby started a grin that turned into a half-moon smile. Glancing at me, he said, "I bet you're wondering what's making me so happy, huh?"

"Yeah, let me in on it."

"Look at all those guys over there watching me. Bet they're wondering how such a funny-looking Jew boy could get so lucky, sittin' here with the young version of Rita

Hayworth." His smile grew wider. "Bet they think I'm either awful rich or awful good."

"That's funny, Bobby, but what they don't know is," and he leaned forward to listen as I said, "I'm in drag!" Bobby's deep laugh seemed to make the men at the other table uncomfortable.

* * *

I'd completed several months of contracts out of town, and I hadn't heard from Bobby in a while. I knew something had to be wrong. At the end of the last engagement, without signed commitments ahead of me, I called his home to see why he hadn't sent the next set of contracts. His wife told me I'd have to be on my own for a while but offered no explanation. After a few weeks I called again, but there was no answer. Finally, I went to his home in Trenton, but the house was closed up. Bobby hadn't been seen or heard from at his hardware store in ages. Weeks passed, and through the grapevine I heard he was selling his interest in the Riviera and the Embassy Club. I made one more effort to call him at home, but the number was no longer in service. Bobby had dropped out of sight, and 10 years would pass before I would find out what happened to him.

With no manager, I booked myself by contacting agents listed in *Billboard*. I drove all over New York and New Jersey lining up jobs. I was driving so much that my legs ached, but that was a minor problem—or so I thought.

In March 1945 I was awakened by the news of an American raid on Tokyo. Everyone was talking about it. It was the most destructive yet of all aggressive raids—low-level incendiary bomb raids on Japanese industrial centers. One month later, on April 12, 1945, the nation was grief-stricken when they heard of the death of President Roosevelt. As Vice President Truman was quickly sworn in, all of America wondered if he could fill Roosevelt's shoes.

The pain in my legs grew worse, but I blamed it on my

overusing the clutch in city driving. A closer analysis, however, told me the pain was more severe during my period.

For years I had been arranging my work schedule around the fourth week of the month. During that week, I'd spend the day in bed, so I could rest enough to be on my feet to do a show at night. Visits to several gynecologists for a hysterectomy only ended in disappointment. Each doctor told me the procedure was against the law unless it was a matter of life or death. And so I continued each month, knees to my chin, rolling from side to side, until one day while doing just that, I felt a lump on my back next to my spine.

After a quick trip to the doctor, I was rushed to the hospital, where they prepared me for exploratory surgery that was to take place the following day; the prognosis was tumors, possibly cancerous. From that moment, everything came so quickly I barely had a chance to panic, and the operation was over before I knew it.

I opened my eyes in the Intensive Care Unit and tried to focus on the two doctors in the room. "You're going to be all right, June," one of them said, patting my shoulder. "There was no cancer."

I was relieved to hear that, but I could tell from his expression that something was wrong. He continued, "We got a scrub bucket full of tumors that were gnarled like fingers around the muscle of your leg, through your body, and protruding next to your spine." He kept patting my shoulder, seemingly worried, which worried me.

"Now, June," he said somberly, "I'm sorry to tell you, in seven hours of surgery we could not save any of your reproductive organs."

"What?" I asked in disbelief.

"I'm so sorry."

"They're all gone?"

"Yes, we tried."

Ignoring his words of consolation, I looked up to the ceiling and with my mind's eye, I saw past the hospital roof and into the heavens, and whispered, "Thank you, God!" I felt smug as a thought crossed my mind: *And I don't even have to shave! Boy, nothing can stop me now.*

Recovering quickly, I returned to work in two weeks and felt better physically than I had in years. And I started meeting new people at new clubs. At one New York club I met Mickey Fuller, a local art dealer, who invited me to a cocktail party he was giving for some—as he put it— "important stars and movie people."

"It'd be good for you to be seen in their company," Mickey said. "Bring a friend if you'd feel more comfortable."

I had occasionally worked with a woman named Jody Barns, who also knew Diana. She was tall and willowy, and though only 17, she had an elegance that belied her youth. She was the envy of many women, as her natural eyelashes were at least a half-inch long. I invited her to come along, and she said yes. I wanted to meet these people, but I had attended a few other cocktail parties and had trouble making small talk. Jody, though, relished the glamour of it all.

Mickey's apartment was on 57th at Park Avenue, and the prestigious address matched the elegance of his guests. In attendance were movie stars we had watched on the screen for years, including Lana Turner, Susan Hayward, and Walter Pidgeon, along with well-known producers and directors, one of whom was Louie B. Mayer. Jody and I were a bit stunned to find ourselves in such famous company, but the evening could prove profitable for both our careers.

"What a break running into Mickey," I whispered to her. "I had no idea he was so influential."

Jody quickly entered into a conversation with one of the guests and soon was seated on a sofa. I wandered around, taking in the scene. The place was wall-to-wall with celebrities. After about an hour, I watched as Walter Pidgeon made his way toward Jody.

As he leaned in to speak to her, he said in his deep, rich voice, "I haven't seen you before. Have we met?" A few minutes into the conversation he remarked, "What beautiful eyes! I've never seen such long lashes in my life. They're real, aren't they?"

Attractive but shy, Jody blushed at the flattery, smiled, and lowered her head. He chatted a bit more. Then he placed his drink on a nearby table, bent down, picked her up from the couch, and carried her across the room. Her expression revealed panic and shock at the brazen behavior of such a distinguished personality. I was aghast at seeing her elevated and transported through the maze of guests with clinking glasses. Other than a slight glance at them going by, no one paid any attention, nor did they seem to hear the bedroom door as it closed.

I rushed to the door and tried the knob, but it was locked. I heard no sound from the other side, so I began knocking and calling but got no answer. Mickey made his way toward me through the crowd. "Don't worry. Pidge won't hurt her," he said, smiling fatherly as he placed a hand on my shoulder.

"Look, I brought her here and I'm responsible," I said.

We both called to the pair in the bedroom but got no answer, not even a sound from Jody. Pounding on the door, I ordered, "Open up or I'll call the police. She's only 17."

In a moment the star opened the door and walked out. I saw Jody, half-dressed, in the dim room.

I picked up her clothes, shoved them at her, and said, "Get dressed. We're leaving."

As we left the party, Louie B. Mayer said quietly, "There's no need to be upset. This kind of thing happens all the time and no harm is done." His words nearly choked me.

Jody and I both felt miserable. What a dismal end to such a promising evening. *What did she do to attract such a disaster?* I asked myself. *Not a damn thing. Why did he do it? To impress the other men? To make the women feel weaker? How insecure he must feel to have to prove his manliness.*

In the car on the way to her hotel, Jody was remorseful and cried briefly, saying it had happened so fast she'd thought he was joking. She was shocked when he began pulling off her clothes, and he was so powerful she couldn't stop him. We talked for some time, until the entire event was behind us.

The following day, Mickey called, saying, "One of my guests was very much taken by your strength of character and honesty and would like to meet you."

"Oh, Mickey," I said, "I'm sorry about last night."

"Hey," he interrupted, "don't worry about it. Look, what are you doing later today? Say, about 4? Could you come to my apartment? This woman really wants to see you."

"Who is it?"

"Lana Turner."

"You're kidding!"

"No, can you make it?"

"Sure, sure, Mickey. I can make it. Damn! See ya at 4." I was flabbergasted and hardly recall anything between the phone call and ringing the bell at the Park Avenue address.

Mickey opened the door wide to welcome me, and I saw the gorgeous Lana Turner sitting across the room.

"Come on in, June," he said. Then, reaching for his hat and coat, he added, "I'm going to leave you two. I've got some running around to do, but make yourselves at home," and he was out the door.

Lana, stunning as ever, was wearing a light-blue silk dress and blue silk shoes. I was too fascinated to move. After she mixed cocktails, I began to relax as we recalled the incident from the evening before. We talked for some time about what was expected in the business and the men who controlled it.

After a second drink, Lana took my hand and led me into the bedroom. Beautiful framed canvases hung on the walls in every available space. Still holding my hand, she sat at the edge of the bed and pulled my blouse from my skirt. Moving toward her, I lost all inhibitions and any awareness of time. Later I recalled hearing soft music playing. She was the epitome of loveliness with her high cheekbones, exquisite body, and flowing blond hair. After our lovemaking, we grew deep into conversation again about the happenings of the night before.

"Now, last night," she said, "you should have just let it pass."

"But Lana, it's not right."

"No, it's not right, but," she warned, "you don't want to make an enemy out of Pidge."

Looking lustfully at the gorgeous woman who lay beside me and thinking only of pleasure, I said, "Who the hell is Pidge?"

Lana laughed and pulled me toward her. "Baby," she said, "you're going to have to give in to some producer or director to get where you're going."

"No, I won't. It's not me."

"Well, just pretend."

"I can't. Don't you understand? Besides, I'll get there, because I'm really good."

Leaning on her elbow, chin resting in her hand, she said in a darling voice, "You're really good, all right, and I haven't even heard you sing."

Embarrassed, I changed the subject back to the night before. "You know, Pidge, as you call him, was wrong. Jody's only 17."

In a kind, sympathetic tone, she said, "Well, baby, it happens all the time."

That was just like Louie B. Mayer's remark the night before: "This kind of thing happens all the time and no harm is done."

And some people have the nerve to look down on me? I thought. *Shame!*

Five

Down Mexico Way

It had been two years since I had heard from my mother. My house in Atlanta was a haven to me. Other than that, home was whatever hotel I happened to be in. I spent my evenings performing, and when I wasn't doing a hospital show, I kept myself busy lining up new engagements.

President Truman had been in office about two and a half months; his biggest objective was ending the war. Most Americans felt bitter toward Japan and supported an American invasion, but Truman's advisers estimated that an invasion would cost about 200,000 U.S. casualties, and he didn't want to risk that loss.

On July 30 I read that a Japanese submarine had sunk the USS Indianapolis. Everyone felt such anger over this—and other atrocities Japan had committed—that one week later, August 6, when Truman gave the order to drop the atomic bomb on Hiroshima, we celebrated. That bombing was followed three days later by the second atomic bomb on Nagasaki, and we celebrated again.

I felt terrible for the innocent people who had lost their lives. They weren't the ones who'd given orders to invade Pearl Harbor, but then we lost many innocent lives there also.

Following the devastation of the bombings, President Truman accepted an unconditional surrender from the Japanese aboard the USS Missouri, named after Truman's home state.

The war was over.

When the news was announced, I was working the Paradise Room at the Henry Grady Hotel in Atlanta. Looking out my dressing-room window, I saw that all of Peachtree Street was becoming a mass of humans. Cars and buses stopped in their tracks, and people ran from their vehicles, from stores and restaurants, dancing and shouting. Loud whistles blew, bells rang, and horns on every vehicle sounded. People cried, and hugged and kissed total strangers, in pandemonium. Overjoyed celebrants climbed lampposts to photograph the crowd. That evening at the Paradise Room, customers bought drinks for other customers, and the chaos lasted until daybreak.

The next day all was quiet, perhaps a result of too much celebrating, but we were happy. Slowly America was getting back to normal.

✳ ✳ ✳

From *Variety and Billboard* I continued to find the names and phone numbers of agents. I spent my days placing calls, delivering photos to agents, and waiting for the phone to ring.

Without my knowledge, Syd Panzer at *The Daily Mirror* in New York sent my photos and résumé to the national Miss Stardust beauty contest. I wasn't overjoyed at the idea of having to parade in high heels and a bathing suit in front of a bunch of guys, but Syd insisted he knew best.

Stardust, Inc., the Stardust Fashion Wear people, sponsored the contest, for which there were 20,000 entrants. As one of the finalists, I'd have to walk down a runway with 10 other women, then try to make the rounds again in heels and a bikini. I couldn't imagine anything worse, nor can I imagine now how I ever ended up a runner-up. But Syd was right. In the contest I modeled the fashions of important clothing and jewelry manufacturers, which resulted in a lot of publicity.

The contest also brought me a celebrity experience of a new and different sort. I received a letter from Aunt Clara, who said that since the contest results were in the Pittsburgh papers, my parents had been receiving phone calls offering congratulations. Two days after receiving her letter I was awakened in the middle of the night by the phone ringing. The man at the other end said he was with *The Pittsburgh Sun-Telegraph.*

"Is this June Walls?" he asked.

"Uh-huh," I mumbled.

"What are your parents' names?"

Half asleep, I said, "I'm sorry, what did you say?"

And I heard, "What is your address in Pittsburgh?"

"Who did you say you were?" I was about to hang up when he apologized for calling so late but said it was an emergency. I listened and answered his questions.

"I had to be positive I had the right person. The Pennsylvania state police received a call from a Mrs. Glenn Walls. Is she your mother?"

"Yes, what's wrong?" I said, completely awake now.

"Were you in a car accident, Miss Walls?"

I sat up like a shot, thinking this was some kind of nightmare. "No, I'm fine. Tell me what happened."

I listened as he continued. "Your mother received a call from a man who said he was a state police officer and that June Walls had been killed in a car accident in New York. He left a number for your mother to call the Pennsylvania state police. He apologized for giving her news of this sort over the phone, then hung up."

"Look, I'm fine," I said calmly. "I haven't been in an accident. It was probably a crank call."

"It may have been, Miss Walls, but your mother is really shaken up, and we suggest that you come home at once. In fact, we'll arrange for your flight, and a police escort will meet you at the Pittsburgh airport."

I called home immediately to find my parents in a state of hysteria. Both of them were so out of control that I left for home as quickly as possible. As soon as I got off the plane a few hours later, my mother screamed and held me tightly, saying she thought she was being punished for telling me she wished I were dead. "Whatever you do, it's all right!" she cried. "As long as you're alive."

When we arrived at the house, Mom and I sat and talked calmly. "June, the way you feel is probably my fault. I'm sure it was the way I raised you."

"Can't you see," I tried to explain, "that it's no one's fault?"

Mom listened, then asked, "But June, how do you know you wouldn't like it if you've never tried it?"

"Look," I said, "I don't have to jump out of a plane to know I wouldn't like skydiving. Our instincts are developed long before we experience them. They're independent of our instructions. We have them, we accept them, and we can't change them—nor should we try."

"But what about the homosexuals who molest children?"

"They're sick, Mom. They're just as sick as people who molest their own children. But you can't condemn all gay people because of the few who are pedophiles. They're in a group of their own and need help."

I could see she was trying hard to understand. She scooted to the edge of her chair and folded her hands on her apron.

"Mom, you believe, as many people do, that this is merely a direction I've decided to take, and between the two sexes I've chosen to be with women. You're wrong, and everyone who believes that is wrong. Hopefully someday scientists will find a biological basis for sexual preference. Until then, am I not supposed to have a mate? Am I not supposed to be attracted to anyone? How unfair."

Wringing her hands tightly, she said, "But Junie, the Bible says it's wrong."

"It also condones slavery," I said. "We've come a long way since the prophets wrote the Bible, and people have found many discrepancies since. And please tell me how all those Bible-reading people can be so judgmental and have so much hatred when the Bible says, 'Judge not...'?"

"They believe they're right, June. Some of them said they were homosexual and then they changed."

"That's what they say," I continued, "and I've met several people who have changed. Some were heterosexual, others were homosexual. The ones I've met have seen both sides because they're bisexual. Often they don't want to admit they could go either way. Sure, I could go through the act—I've had many opportunities to do just that. But sex has to be more than an act; I have to feel something for the person."

My mother held my face in her hands, and I wanted so much to be everything she wanted me to be. It would have been much more rewarding to grit my teeth, let Mighty Mite have his fun, and be a star in a Broadway show. But the mere thought of having intimate relations with a man made me ill.

My mother could only look at me sadly and say, "But Junie, you're so beautiful that it's hard for me to believe."

"I won't spend the rest of my life the way the majority thinks I should, based on what they see," I said. "If I did, God would never forgive me, because I would be committing an injustice to every honest fiber of my being."

She seemed to be hearing me for the first time. "I never really thought of it that way, June," she said, "but I'm beginning to understand, and I'm so thankful you're alive."

After that, my mother never mentioned the subject again. The police investigation of the crank call turned up nothing. In the end, we put it down as a horrible incident, born out of a sick mind. But I was grateful for the renewed relationship with my mother. Once again I had her love, and we were closer than ever.

While I was home, Dad gave me a stack of mail he had

planned to forward. There was mail from friends I had met and a card from Mingo, a letter from Florence and Betty in the Philippines, but nothing from Diana. The message was clear. I couldn't dwell on my sadness but knew my love for her would never change.

My overnight visit to Pittsburgh allowed me to see first-hand how hard my parents were working; they needed more help. But living expenses in New York were taking nearly all my extra money, so I had little to send home. I recalled that several agents had said that although New York had a lot of work, Mexico was where the real money was, so when I returned to New York, I accepted a contract in Mexico City. Anticipating a problem with transporting Pammie across the border, I sent her home to Pittsburgh.

* * *

The year was 1947. I was 23 and looking forward to my new contract at Ciro's, *the* swank club in the Hotel Reforma in Mexico City. Mr. A.C. Blumenthal, manager of Ciro's, whom they called Blumie, had hired me, saying that Mexicans were very receptive to Americans. I was on my way to meeting a new kind of audience.

When my plane landed in Mexico City, I was greeted by a mariachi band. Mr. Blumenthal's chauffeur was also at the foot of the stairs as I descended from the plane. He ushered me to a limousine, where Mr. Blumenthal waited.

"*Señorita* Walls?" he inquired. "Welcome to Mexico City!" As we drove to the Hotel Reforma I noticed the vibrant colors throughout the city: reds were bright reds, whites were stark, pinks were shocking, and the people were happy, always smiling. Coming from the "rush rush" of New York, I considered this laid-back contrast delightful. Since much of Mexico's income depended upon American tourism, people from the States were treated with warm hospitality. The moment we arrived at the Reforma, Blumie invited me to attend a bullfight with him Sunday afternoon.

At the Plaza de México, the attendance numbered from 30,000 to 40,000 people. The opening procession was bright and colorful, as sunlight danced from each matador's sequin-trimmed suit of lights.

Blumie and his friends explained the details of the fight as it progressed. "There are three elements to a fight: the cape work, the *banderillas*, and the *muleta* and sword. After the preliminary cape work, the *banderillas*, which are decorated barbed darts, are thrust into the bull's neck."

I cringed at that, but then Blumie explained, "As with right- or left-handed people, a bull tends to hook to the right or left, and this must be corrected. Otherwise it would be a massacre for the matador. The *banderilla*, placed in the proper side, pricks the skin, with more discomfort than pain, and this encourages him to charge in a straight line."

Blumie pointed to a picture on the cover of the program he held. "See, June, a fighting bull has a small triangular head with wide horns curving forward. The neck is short, with heavy muscles. When he's angry, the muscles are erect. Notice the wide shoulders? Most of his weight is over his front feet. Now, keep in mind, they're bred to fight anything that moves."

Captivated by the spectacle, I attended the bullfight every Sunday. Traveling to and from the fights, boys would jump in front of cars, waving sweaters or shirts in imitation of the matador's passes. Each Sunday I felt more and more drawn to the ring, until in my mind I was putting myself in the matador's place.

In addition, I began making many new friends. One in particular was Vincente Calderon, an accomplished pianist who performed with me. Without conversation on the subject, Vincente understood my sexual orientation from the beginning. With the air cleared from the get-go, we had a terrific friendship. Many times I'd be dressed to do a show, and he'd look me up and down, shake his head, and say, "My, my, what a shame!" That remark was always followed by a good laugh from both of us. Besides working together at the Reforma, we performed on radio shows and at a command performance for Presidente Miguel Alemán Valdés.

Mexicans seemed to accept homosexuals more readily than most Americans did. Lacking feminine mannerisms, onstage I moved slowly, to keep from looking like a butch in sequins. And, making the most of it, I never had a problem.

Days and nights in Mexico became more glamorous as time passed. The nightclubs, theaters, people, music, bullfights, and reporters—all combined to create a marvelous life for me. I loved Mexico and was growing to love its people. While singing at Ciro's at the Reforma, between shows I'd sing in the Champagne Room at the same hotel. It was a small, intimate room that sat about 75 people, with large paintings by Diego Rivera covering the walls. It was the kind of room where a singer can perform directly to individuals in the audience. My only accompaniment was Vincente at the piano and one violinist. We created moods the guests absolutely loved. Sometimes we worked into the night doing special requests, and the guests would remain until the wee hours of the morning. The consumption of many cocktails often prompted a warm, receptive audience who made one request after another. I honored all the requests except the truly heterosexual ones like "The Man That Got Away," "The Man I Love," and so forth, because I never sang a lyric I couldn't feel.

* * *

Several months had passed when I received a letter from Jody, Diana's friend, saying that Diana was now married. I was terribly saddened. Until that time I had harbored glimmers of hope that perhaps someday we'd be together, but now it was time to stop dreaming and put that part of my life behind me. I could never forget her, though. *Something must have happened*, I told myself. *She never would have done this on her own.*

Diana and I had shared something special, and many times I found myself looking for her in a crowd on the street, at the club, or in a restaurant. Seeing her, I'd suddenly feel warm inside and rush toward her, only to discover it was a look-alike.

But Mexico, with its charming, sometimes promiscuous women, eased my pain greatly. Following my shows in the Champagne Room, many times I'd return to my hotel room and find a girl waiting for me. A familiar face from the audience. Obviously they were seeing through my sequined façade.

One such time I found the most gorgeous, voluptuous platinum blond lying naked in my bed.

"How did you get in here?" I asked, shock written across my face.

With no more modesty than a newborn, she sat straight up and proclaimed, "The bellboy!"

Quickly moving toward the bed, I grabbed for the sheet to cover her. "Who are you?" I demanded.

Holding my forearms tightly, she pulled me onto the bed beside her. "Shelli da Cordona, your new cousin," she said. "I told the desk clerk I wanted to surprise you, and they let me in. From there it was easy. He just opened the door."

Women were everywhere. Many times they were masculine women who failed to see through the sequins. Some were extremely flirty, but I didn't know if they were serious or just curious. But none of them could fill the void I felt. They could only keep me busy, so that I'd have little time to dwell on the past. At least that's what I kept telling myself.

One evening a gorgeous woman requested "Mam'selle," which is a man's song. Seated with a gentleman, she was wearing a black gown with a plunging neckline and a long strand of pearls. She was refined grace.

In answering her request I worked the entire room. As was my custom, as I approached each table I stood at the back of a gentleman, with my hand on his shoulder, and directed the song to the lady at the table. The men never objected, and the women loved the attention. That evening a woman had made the request, so I finished the song at her table.

During the applause, the gentleman asked me to join them after the show. He presented himself as Tony Fredressa and introduced the lovely lady as Alta Rae Slone. She was an exquisite combination of dark eyes, blond hair, and splendid features. I learned that Tony was a member of the board of the Banco de México and that the woman had been a show-girl with the Earl White Reviews. She had come to Mexico with the company and chose to remain in Mexico City. She loved the easy way of living in Mexico and spoke both Spanish and English fluently.

Meticulously dressed, Tony was trim and sharp, with dark hair and a small mustache. He also spoke perfect English. We three spent one of those memorable evenings that I hated to see end.

Shortly after returning to my room, the phone rang. It was Alta Rae Slone. "I just wanted to tell you how utterly fascinating I find you," she said, "and I would like very much to see you for a cocktail alone. Could that be arranged?" After having been completely enthralled with her all evening, I had to make an effort to keep from sounding too excited.

The following day, arriving early at the cocktail lounge, I was seated with a full view of the entrance. Alta appeared, looking exquisite. During our conversation over cocktails, I learned that she was living in a room in the home of a Mexican family on the outskirts of the city. She had been looking for a job, possibly as a model, since she had previously worked as one. She was 26, three years my senior. She hated cold weather, loved calla lilies, and was a charming flirt. After asking a question, she'd flatter me by appearing completely engrossed by the simplest answer.

After talking a while, she grew quiet, as though debating something. I studied her as she stirred her drink. Then she popped the question point-blank: "Are you a homosexual?"

I didn't know whether to laugh or continue sitting there with my mouth open. It was so unexpected.

"Well, are you?"

"That's what they tell me."

"Well, are you?" she insisted.

"If you're talking about me physically," I said, "as a woman, most definitely. But if you're talking about my mind, I feel as normal as that guy over there, who's obviously trying to charm the woman he's with. If he were sitting there looking like a girl, it wouldn't necessarily change his way of thinking, would it? He'd still want the same thing, regardless of how he looked."

"I was sure of it, June. But not Tony—you had him fooled last night. It would be difficult for anyone to tell, because I can't imagine a more beautiful body than yours."

"Oh, God, Alta," I said with disgust, "look at me in here. Look at the one who's looking at you through these eyes!"

"Yes," she said, "that's how I could tell! It was the way you looked at me. I knew it right away by the look in your eyes."

She sat quietly, smiling, studying me for the longest time. Finally, she spoke of a quaint hotel called La Cañada, about an hour's drive from the city.

"I'd love to go there with you," she said. "Can you arrange for a night off?"

My contract had just been renewed for another month. "Perhaps on a slow night Blumie wouldn't mind."

The following Monday, Alta picked me up at the hotel. I remember the narrow roadway winding around the mountainside and thick greenery nearly touching the car as we drove. We passed children along the road selling everything from Coca-Cola to cowhides. Because of the high altitude, the temperature during the day was usually 25 degrees warmer than at night. It was a perfect day for a drive.

After an hour or so on the road, we motored up the drive to La Cañada. Our room was huge and furnished with old Spanish wrought iron and white fur rugs. A stone fireplace in the center of the room held logs and dry sticks, in preparation for another chilly night.

Alta and I dined on a private terrace overlooking miles of terrain. Ribbon-like paths divided the vegetation on the mountains, with little burros toting backpacks and boys slowly making their way around the mountain trail. La Cañada was everything Alta had said it would be.

We listened to the strains of mariachis while absorbing the warmth of each other's company. As the evening began to cool, we went inside and lit the fireplace, which cast a warm glow over the room. I watched as Alta moved about, captivating me with every step. She had a devilish way of turning her head and a nearly childlike smile.

I left the room to slip into something more comfortable. When I returned, Alta, in a pale blue negligee, lay on the white fur rug enjoying the warmth of the fireplace. Smiling slightly, she made space for me beside her. When a woman wants you, you know it. The look was unmistakable, and I was bewitched. As I lay beside her, she turned toward me and loosened the ribbon ties on her gown straps. They fell softly, like leaves in late summer, finding private little places to hang on, only to shift again. I tasted the corners of her lips and all of her, and touched her as though I were without sight and wanted to remember it always. She held a mystic charm that left me without the aid of my senses or thought or reason, as the embers in the fireplace burned low and time had no meaning.

The crackling of the fire awakened me much later. I draped my arms around Alta—tenderly, so as not to disturb her—and she slept on.

After breakfast the next morning, Alta was even more exciting. She wore the glow of romance well. But it was time to leave our romantic hideaway and get back to the rest of the world.

Alta wanted to look for an apartment in Mexico City, which would probably take several days, and I would be busy with rehearsals and working up new songs. Several days passed before she called, terribly happy. "I've got a job modeling," she said, "and I found a darling apartment. I want you to see it. I'll be there in 10 minutes!"

Arriving promptly, she picked me up, and we drove to a place on Michelet, a residential street. Through her living room window, I took in the panoramic view of the Avenida de la Reforma, a monument with an angel on top, in the center of the Avenue. Alta was happy, making plans for furniture, draperies, and the like. "I've got several modeling shows to do, and I want you to see some of them," she said, sounding as though she was going to be extremely busy with her new life.

We were together every other day for weeks. Alta's work was unpredictable; she said she never knew when she'd be hired on a show in Acapulco or California or Texas. In the meantime, my contract was extended for another three months.

As the weeks passed, I was growing more infatuated with Alta. The longer I knew her, the more I respected her intelligence and beauty and the way she cleverly combined the two. It soon became obvious that, because of this talent, she had an "in" with influential people, a trait I found helpful, particularly on one occasion.

I'd been in the country six months when the Mexican authorities "reminded" me that my work permit had expired. In fact, they weren't going to allow me to perform that night. To renew the permit I'd have to travel to Brownsville, Tex., and back, which meant setting aside a great deal of time for driving, missing work, and filing my papers. I told Alta, who said, "I'll handle it. Don't worry." She made a brief phone call, then turned to me and said, "See? It's all arranged. We'll leave in an hour. El Banco de México is flying us to Brownsville with a money shipment."

And sure enough, the entire floor of the plane was covered with bags of money and gold, and we walked over the heaps of bagged cash! We arrived, renewed my permit, and returned on the same plane, the same day. "See?" she said, looking devilish. "It pays to know the right people."

Many times she invited me to watch her fashion shows,

and many nights she'd be at Ciro's with several fine-looking gentlemen. When we were alone she'd ask me through a sneaky, crooked smile, "Are you jealous?"

"Of course I'm jealous!" I'd tell her.

"Good! That makes it interesting." Then she'd smile that darling, fiendish smile that thrilled me. She was a pro, and I the novice.

Soon after, I had to leave the country for a six-month contract in the States. When I returned to Mexico with a new contract at Ciro's, Alta greeted me at the airport, smiling from ear to ear. Time had changed nothing.

Alta helped me unpack at the hotel. Then, taking my hand, she said, "I want you to see my apartment! Get a change of clothing and something to lounge in to keep at my place. Please stay with me tonight." I could think of nothing I wanted more.

Bursting with excitement, she opened her apartment door to reveal elegant, expensive furnishings. Clearly, money was no longer a problem.

"Make yourself comfortable, darling," Alta said as we entered, then she called into another room, "Maria, please bring us two cocktails."

"Maria?"

"Yes, you will meet her."

Moments later a small woman, dressed in a maid's uniform, appeared with two drinks.

"So, this is Maria," I said. "Alta, it's wonderful you're doing so well with your career."

She ignored my remark and instead moved about the room, looking hard in my direction. She'd sip her drink and look. Finally, she sat beside me, one arm on the back of the couch.

"What are you staring at?" I asked curiously.

"Wait a minute, dear." After studying me a bit longer, she said, "Your nose is just a little too round at the end."

Laughing, I pushed her hand from my face.

"No, no, wait." She turned my head sideways. "Really, why don't you let me make some calls? If I could set something up, would you have your nose done?"

This was so ridiculous, but hell, I didn't care. "Alta," I said, "if that's what you want, that's what you'll get!"

She gathered my information and made an appointment for the surgery to take place at the end of my engagement at Ciro's. The doctor informed us that someone would have to care for me for a week or two after I left the hospital, especially as there was a risk of postsurgery hemorrhaging. Also, I'd have to return every day to have the bandages changed.

"No problem," she told him. "June can stay with me."

The date was set, and I was so grateful that I sent Alta a large bouquet of calla lilies.

When the day of the surgery arrived, Alta waited at the hospital. Afterward, I looked like a mummy with all the bandages covering my head, and I could barely speak. As the days passed, the stench from the dried blood worsened. Finally, I was released early, since Alta had assured the doctor that she would take care of me.

As she drove me back from the hospital, I muttered, "Wait! You missed the turn-off to your apartment."

"No, I didn't," she said. "I have to drop you off at your hotel. I'm busy tonight."

"But you told the doctor—"

"You'll be all right until tomorrow, won't you?"

"No, I won't. Don't do this, Alta."

She stopped the car anyway and let me out in front of the hotel. I was a sight, and the pain was worsening by the minute.

Two days passed, and I hadn't heard from Alta. Tony Fredressa called to ask how I was.

"OK, I guess," I said.

"Is Alta with you?"

"I was supposed to be staying with her, but I can't get in touch with her. I don't know where she is or what's happened to her. I'm really worried."

"Don't worry about her," he said flatly. "She'll take care of herself. She's not worth your time."

"What do you mean?"

"Just forget her. She's not worth it."

"I can't forget her. I'm too involved with her," I said.

Tony took a deep breath then exhaled. "I didn't want to tell you this, but seeing the position you're in, I must. Alta's been involved with every man in Mexico City. Forget her—she's bad for you."

"Tony! Do you know what you're saying?"

"I know what I'm saying. I didn't want to tell you but...well..."

"What? You didn't want to tell me what?"

"Alta is a high-paid, high-class prostitute."

I was stunned. "My God, Tony, you must be wrong. She cares about me. I know she does. You've got to be wrong."

"Yeah, she cares about you and 50 other guys."

My brain was racing. "How do you know they've been with her? Maybe they're just bragging."

"I wish I could tell you that, June, but I know better."

"But Alta was with me every day or, well, every other day," I argued. "She didn't have time for that. She was always occupied with something—modeling, furnishing her apartment..."

"She wasn't with you when you were working at night, was she? What about those special trips to Acapulco for fashion shows? And how do you think she was able to get you on the Bank of Mexico plane? She knows the right people, June, because she's been with them all."

"Oh, Tony, you've got to be wrong."

"Find out for yourself," he said. "Tell you what I'll do—I'll call you at the right time and you hurry over to her apartment."

I heard the click of the phone as he hung up. I felt numb and lost all awareness of time. Night came, then daylight. I was incapable of any emotional expression.

Night came again, and I was jolted back to reality by the

sound of the phone ringing. It was Tony. "June, listen, have you heard from Alta?"

"Not yet."

"Well, go to her apartment and see for yourself. Go now."

I ran out of my room, flagged a cab, went to Alta's, and asked the driver to wait.

Maria answered the ring of the bell. "*¿Sí?*"

"Maria? *Señorita* Alta? *Esta es* June."

"*No aquí, señorita. No está.*"

"Open the door!" I yelled.

Maria cracked the door slightly. I slipped my foot inside, pushed her aside, and ran upstairs, two steps at a time. "No, no, *señorita*," Maria cried, following me. "No, no!" I found Alta in the living room. Passing her, I darted into the bedroom, and there stood a half-dressed son of a bitch. Alta ran after me.

"What is this, Alta? Who is this guy? Why are you doing this?" She was silent for a long time. Then I said, "Get this guy out of here!"

Finally, she spoke. "I'm sorry."

"Alta, this fellow is leaving!"

"No, you're the one who's leaving."

For a moment, I was deadened by the sound of her words. "I thought I meant something to you," I said. "You were with me constantly. How did *he* get into the picture?"

"You'll be leaving Mexico, June, going back to your life, and this...this my life."

"Why did you let me get so hooked on you? So involved?" I knew I looked terrible in all those bandages. I was absolutely mortified, reduced to nothing.

I left, taking only my sadness with me. I was crouched to enter the backseat of the cab when I heard Alta call from a second-floor window, "Wait, you forgot a couple of things!" As I looked up, I saw my underwear, a suit, pajamas, and a half-dozen calla lilies flying from the window, floating down to the hood of the cab and onto the street. I started for them, but the driver, seeing the state I was in, said, *"No, señorita, el coche,"* motioning for me to get in the cab. He kindly gathered my clothing and placed it beside me.

In the privacy of my room, I wanted to cry out. First Diana and now this. The pain was suffocating, making it hard for me to breathe. The doctor had told me not to bend over for fear of hemorrhaging, so I lay on my back, and the tears soaked the bandages all the way to the back of my neck.

After a while the pressure was gone and I could think more clearly.

The phone rang. It was Tony.

"This is so hard to believe," I told him.

"That's where the furniture and beautiful clothes came from," he said, sympathy underlying his voice. "That's why she can afford the luxurious apartment. The trips out of town for fashion shows—those were all lies. She was working, but not the way you thought. Oh, she had a few shows, but they're really a front. All her gentleman friends also believe she's a full-time model."

As he spoke, my hurt turned to fury at being so cleverly deceived, and finally I became angry enough to say, "By damn, Tony, there is one consolation. All those guys are paying for something I was getting for free."

The bandages were drying, and I had time to think. The men I had met in the past weren't the only rotten ones in the world—some of the women were too. *They'll all knife me in the back if I give them the chance,* I thought. *The only difference is a woman will do it with a smile and use a thinner blade.*

∗ ∗ ∗

After the bandages were removed, I returned to Pittsburgh. Unfortunately, I needed six months to recuperate, but it would give me some time to spend with Pammie. She helped divert my mind from Alta. For some time my dog had been losing her hearing, and I had no idea how far it had deteriorated. She stayed very close to my side while I was with her. Pammie was retired from show business, but I could never forget how she had enhanced my career. She was like a child to me, loyal and mindful of my wishes.

Whenever I said "stay" she stayed, but one afternoon while I was visiting a neighbor across the street, Pammie came looking for me. She saw me leave the neighbor's house and ran in my direction, just as she had once scurried across the stage. The poor little dog couldn't hear a sound, much less the truck barreling down the road. I screamed for her to stop, but her eyes never left me as she raced headlong into the truck. As my dear friend died in my arms, a part of me went with her.

It's incredibly difficult to lose a beloved pet. Pammie was a special friend, and losing her was particularly painful. Nothing could console me; I just needed time. Some may say she was only a pet, but the shock of having her life taken, in an instant, compelled me to make every moment of my life a direct move forward.

✳ ✳ ✳

It was time to get back to singing, so I contacted an agent, who booked me into the Mayflower Hotel in Akron, Ohio. It felt good to be working again, and I did so with more perseverance than ever.

The war was over, but I continued to entertain at Navy, Army, and Air Force bases and at hospitals whenever needed. After each performance, service people came to thank me, many of whom were "family."

In New York I signed a one-year contract with the biggest agency in town. The agent assigned to me phoned the day after I signed, saying he had a contract for me that I had to pick up at his apartment. Arriving at the address he had given me, I knocked on the door, and a deep voice said, "Come in."

When I opened the door, the agent came toward me with his hand extended. "Hi, June, nice to meet you," he smiled. "The contract is over there." He pointed to a desk across the room and motioned for me to go in that direction. At the desk, I picked up the contract and began reading. Suddenly I felt him standing close to my back. With his hands on my waist, he turned me around and pressed his hips to mine. "We're gonna be good together, June," he said, pulling me closer.

I was aghast. My body stiffened as I tried to push him away. "Come on, June, relax," he said.

I crumpled the contract, shoved it into his smiling mouth, and said, "Stick it."

Rushing from the building, I was furious. *So,* I thought, *there goes another bastard,* and I was resigned to the fact that the world was full of them.

✻ ✻ ✻

After working with Lou Perry and Bobby Cohen, I knew what a good agent was supposed look like. In every large city I had between five and 50 agents from which to choose. But once you sign with a bad agent, he can do absolutely nothing and still collect 15% of your receipts. At every club, agents in the audience would come backstage and offer me an exclusive contract. But I was choosy; if they weren't connected with the best clubs, I wouldn't sign.

The large nightclubs had their own theatrical agents, who collected 15% of the salary of every act working in the club, regardless of who booked the act. Therefore, I'd call the best clubs, get the name of their agent, and call him. That way, I paid only one 15% commission, directly to the club's agent.

Unable to find a decent long-term agent, I booked my own acts in 1948, 1949, and 1950 by calling agents at the big clubs and setting dates. I worked relentlessly, seven days a week, with no time off. I'd travel all night to begin each new engagement and worked every major city in the eastern United States with a large theater or nightclub. Return engagements brought even bigger salaries. I was making professional progress, and

1950 glamour shot
of me at age 26

Clockwise from above:
- At home in Pennsylvania at age 15 with one of my pups
- At home in Atlanta with Sheika in 1947
- With Grandma (left) and her friend in 1956
- Proud new owner of my second convertible, a 1955 Chevy Bel Air
- The look they wanted

Opposite page: Publicity shot taken at the Hotel Reforma in Mexico City in 1947
This page: Performing at a gig at Grossinger's Hotel and Resort in the Catskills in 1955

Clockwise from opposite page:
- In my gold and white *traje de luces* in 1956
- Preparing for my first bullfight in San Miguel Allende, Mexico
- My trusty *cuadrilla*
- Executing a *Gaonera* pass
- Performing a *pase derechazo*

Practicing the Veronica pass
in Mexico City, 1956

my status as a performer had improved enough to increase my salary to a degree where I could pay for my own accompanist.

I called Vincente Calderon in Mexico City, and he agreed to join me for the next two contracts in Havana and Ciudad Trujillo, previously called Santo Domingo, in the Dominican Republic. Vincente wore jackets that matched my gowns, which made for a classy-looking act. He was a fine person, both onstage and off. Working with new arrangements of Spanish and Mexican songs, he explained each phrase, enabling me to place emphasis on the correct words.

In the Dominican Republic I was scheduled to sing at the Hotel Jaragua. The setting of the hotel was outstanding. Its beauty alone made singing there a rare pleasure. The ballroom was outdoors, and the background for the bandstand resembled a huge seashell sitting upright with its back to the Caribbean. People were packed to capacity night after night throughout the run of the show. Management and critics called the engagement an "overwhelming success," and we left with a promise to return.

Havana, my next contract, was an exciting place before Castro took over, cosmopolitan with a distinct international flavor. We played at the Hotel National and were well received, but everyday living was difficult. It was nearly impossible to get a bellboy, cab, or room service. And Cubans seemed to resent Americans; we both felt it. When our contract ended, we were glad to move on to our next gig in Mexico City.

It was terrific being back at Ciro's and meeting all the celebrities who were vacationing or working in Mexico, people like Tyrone Power and Linda Christian. Tyrone had just finished shooting *Captain From Castille*. The film featured one scene in particular with harlequin Great Danes running in a field. After hearing of my desire to own a Dane, Tyrone gave me the name and number of the film's animal handler. With his help I acquired one of the puppies, a fierce-looking dog I named Sheika.

Of course, I couldn't keep a Great Dane in a hotel room, so I had to keep Sheika in a kennel until I returned to the States. So she would get to know me, I spent each day taking a cab to the kennel, then driving to Chapultepec Park to let her romp and exercise. With no one else in my life, Sheika was good company.

Alta was rarely at the club, but when she was, I was incapable of speaking to her with ease. I knew it was over, though, and at least the hurt was gone.

Nightly, the club was packed. Critics called me "The Inimitable June Walls" and "Emotions in Song." A local magazine, *México al Día,* sported my picture on the cover. Because of good publicity, business prospered.

Blumie introduced me to many interesting people. After one especially responsive show, he sent a waiter to escort me to a large table of guests sitting ringside. Once there, I recognized Rita Hayworth and Prince Ali Kahn and was introduced to Margaret Mitchell, author of *Gone With the Wind.* I was so impressed, I had to struggle to keep my composure. I recalled the performance I had just given and felt grateful for the blinding spotlights. If I'd known so many celebrities were watching, I would've been a pile of nerves. Miss Hayworth was painfully beautiful.

After the introductions, I was seated between Valerie Black, a lovely woman about 50 years old, and Margaret Mitchell. Mrs. Mitchell, dressed in a neatly tailored suit, was unimposing and proper. I confessed to her how privileged I felt to be invited to a table of such celebrities. With kind humility she asked questions about my career and how I spent my days. After hearing about Sheika, she said, "I'd love to go to the park with you tomorrow. If you like, I'll pick you up at the hotel."

"That sounds wonderful," I replied, flattered and amazed by her invitation.

"It would be my pleasure. What time would be best for you?"

"I've been leaving the hotel around 10."

"Fine, I'll pick you up at 10. You know, I too am an early riser and my mornings are often boring."

I felt pleased to have a new friend—and Margaret Mitchell, at that!

Valerie Black, the attractive wife of the president of a large bank in Boston, was also extremely friendly. She was wearing a beaded gown, dangling diamond earrings, and a white ermine coat casually draped over her shoulders. Valerie, as she asked to be called, was lively, almost to the point of being pushy. "I love that magazine cover photo of you, June," she cooed. "In fact, that's what brought me here. I had to see if you were just as beautiful in person. And you are."

"Thank you, Valerie. How sweet of you."

"Tell me about your life," she went on, "and I'm very interested in your act."

I spent the rest of the evening answering questions and admiring Rita Hayworth from across the table.

Miss Hayworth and her husband, Prince Ali Kahn, left Mexico a few days later, but I became fast friends with Valerie Black and Margaret Mitchell. I spent several days with the famous author. Her chauffeur would drive us to the kennel, where we'd pick up Sheika, and then drop us off at Chapultepec Park. Sheika would go off on a healthy trot while I enjoyed the company of this charming lady. We'd lunch at noon and have long conversations about her work.

"Writing is a lonely life, dear," Mrs. Mitchell said. "You have to wait many years for your applause, and then it often doesn't happen."

"I don't think I could stand the wait," I told her.

"Yes, you could. The most important thing is time. The work is so engrossing, but you never have enough time."

Mrs. Mitchell was seldom seen at nightspots; in contrast, Valerie could be found at a ringside table nightly. Strong-willed, Valerie blatantly expressed her opinion at any cost.

"I should've been your mother," she told me. "Then I could mold you into what you should be."

Each show she studied my performance and gave a nod of approval or disapproval. "It's amazing," she said. "You mesmerize both the men in the audience and the women. Tell me, June, what do you think you look like to an audience?"

I could only answer with raised eyebrows and a laugh. Still, it made me think. I had learned much about entertaining from other entertainers, and it was working well. But I always felt a little like the boy next door, in a dress singing.

"Answer me, June," she prodded. "Pretend you're watching your act."

"Well, I try to look and sing as best I can and put some inner part of me into each lyric. That's it. My biggest goal is to give the best performance possible. I think I come across as a good singer, mmm, and, I suppose, sincere."

"Really, now," she said, with an air of superiority.

"Really."

Valerie studied me. Then she removed her earrings and bracelets, two-inch-wide filigree bands of diamonds. "In your next show start with a blackout, walk to the mike, then bring up the lights. Stand there for a moment without singing. Take your time." She handed me her jewels. "Do me a favor. Put these on for your next show, and this," she said, reaching for her fur coat, "put this on one shoulder. Now, do as I say. And take those damn combs out of your hair, fluff it way out, and let's see what happens."

Feeling as though I didn't look feminine enough, onstage I was accustomed to approaching the mike in the same manner I'd handed a customer a loaf of bread when I was a kid: "Here it is! You're gonna love it!" So I wondered what difference Valerie's suggestions would make.

With my new props in hand, I went to my room to change for the last show and fixed myself a drink. *More feminine, huh?* I thought. *That's what they all want.* I had a second drink and then a third. Little by little, the alcohol took over and camouflaged the person inside. I selected the Chinese red gown, added Valerie's diamonds and white fur, fluffed out my hair, and stood before the mirror.

"Well!" I said to my reflection. "You're looking more girly all the time. I hardly recognize you in there. But if this is what they want, let's give it to 'em."

Out of the room we went, me and whomever they thought I was.

The club lights dimmed to a blackout and were followed by the words, "Ladies and gentlemen, the incomparable *Señorita* June Walls." My theme music, "Full Moon and Empty Arms," began building. The white fur dripped from one shoulder. In total darkness during the applause, I walked center stage to the mike; the spotlight came up, and I waited. A stillness hovered over the room, a hush that seemed to interrupt their breathing. I stood looking at the audience, ready to begin, and it happened. Like magic, applause spread until the room was full of sound. They were standing, smiling, applauding for the outside shell. I couldn't help wondering if they'd applaud if they knew the real me.

When the sound subsided, I said sadly, "Now I know what you want." That too was taken the wrong way. Once again they responded, and the audience was mine.

After the show I went to my room and leaned against the door. I saw my reflection in the window across my room. "We sure had 'em fooled tonight, didn't we?" I said. "We gave 'em something to look at and nobody knew I was in there."

Piece by piece, the evening clothes came off. Heels and eyelashes lay beside me. A much nicer person surfaced, a more humble one who loved deeply and wanted so much to be accepted. I was beginning to understand what the public wanted. I had been trying to convince myself that they liked my voice. It hurt to think that the disguise was so important. After that, I needed two or three stiff drinks before each show to make the person inside disappear. That way I could forget I was in there. After a couple of drinks, I could accept the façade. I was making good money, but every day was Halloween.

Valerie never missed a show. After each one she insisted that I sit with her table of influential friends. She was forceful, somewhat like a mother. Still, I humored her. But I kept the daytime for Mrs. Mitchell, Sheika, and myself.

* * *

I attended several bullfights and met the renowned matador Carlos Arruza, a brave man and talented artist. I simply could not get enough. At the fights, the glamour of my work was gone, and I could be myself. Like thousands of excited Mexicans who filled arenas throughout the country, I attended the event every Sunday at 4 P.M. I went with Blumie and constantly asked questions about the art, as though I had a desire to participate someday.

"The bull gets his stature from his father and his courage from his mother," he explained. "A cowardly bull is dangerously unpredictable in the ring, so it's vital that the heifers intended for breeding be tested for courage. The testing is called a *tienta*. Two-year-old heifers are worked with a *muleta*—a red, semicircular wool flannel cloth draped over a 24-inch stick called a *palillo*—and a cape. The animals are coaxed to charge the cloth. They'll either bravely continue to charge or shy away in cowardice. The cowardly ones are ultimately sent to market. The brave ones bear bulls for the ring."

Tientas, Blumie went on to explain, are celebrations with food, wine, and music. The invited guests may be celebrities or politicians, and professional or even amateur bullfighters. Those with enough nerve take turns at testing the spirit and courage of the animals.

On one occasion Blumie invited me to a *tienta* at Pastaje, the ranch of Carlos Arruza. Many aficionados claimed that Arruza was the best and most versatile matador of all time. To be invited to his home was a rare privilege.

Arruza was gracious with his answers to my many questions

about the art of bullfighting. "No, no, *señorita*, the bull is never trained. He is reared in rocky terrain to toughen his hooves and on hills to build sinew. *Vaqueros* (cowboys) are always on horseback. The first time the bull sees a man on foot is when it enters the ring to fight."

"You mean, the bull never sees a man on foot even as it's bred?" I asked.

"That's right. It only sees men on horseback until it enters the ring."

I began to appreciate why breeding courageous heifers was so important. The contest was between brute force and intellect. The more I learned, the more intrigued I became.

One after another, guests entered the ring. It wasn't unusual to see celebrities try the heifers. Some of the impromptu matadors were experienced and made beautiful passes with the cape. These passes were named after the matadors who had created them, such as the *Gaonera* created by Gaona, the *Manoletina* created by Manolete, the *Arrucina* created by Arruza, and so on. The *remate* is a pass that takes the lure away rapidly, in order to stop the heifer momentarily.

From where Blumie and I were sitting, I had a clear view of Ava Gardner dressed in a short black jacket and *corteba* hat. She looked absolutely stunning, conversing with several bullfighters, all eyes on her. Full of life, she anxiously made her way through the crowd and down the steps, only to stop for a moment behind the *barrera*, the safety barrier. She appeared quite confident. When offered the heifer to test, she walked into the ring with great stature and poise, but I was afraid for her. Once in the ring, she called the heifer. Lightning-fast, the animal's head turned, throwing saliva onto the sand as she came charging toward Ava. With a cape, she directed the calf to charge and pass around her body, with a well-executed Veronica pass. The crowd went crazy.

"She's good, Blumie!" I said cheering.

Ava's figure was a silhouette of black against the sand, with the sun hitting the wide brim of her hat. Her performance elicited an outburst of *"olé"* from every spectator. The excitement mounted as I watched.

If only I could do that, I thought. I knew I wouldn't look as good, but what the heck—we were both the same height, weight, and build. If she could do it, I could too, and what a challenge it would be to control such a strong force. Blumie must have caught on to my fascination as he asked, "Want to try?"

"Oh, yeah!" I answered without hesitation.

Blumie signaled a ranch hand and asked him for a cape and permission for me to enter the ring. I jumped to my feet when another small animal entered, and edged my way toward the *barrera* knowing I was the one to test her. She looked spunky. Walking carefully into the ring, I stopped where I'd seen the others before me stop. Then I inched my way along, with nothing to go on but gut instinct and my hundreds of hours of observation on Sunday afternoons.

"Uh-hah!" I called, imitating the others, to get the heifer's attention. The knot in my throat made it difficult to swallow.

"Uh-hah, *torita!*" The animal weighed several hundred pounds, and I damn well didn't want to be hit by that. Again I called. She looked straight at me. One slight move of the cape and she started. I timed the cape ahead of her as she barreled past me. She was so fast that there wasn't time to think before she was back. I stepped out again, innocently confident because I was still standing.

The other guests were happily egging me on, so back and forth we moved. The calf was good. Finally, I attempted the best *remate* I could and walked from the ring. The heifer had shown no fear. Several ranch hands, knowing she would be excellent for breeding, lifted her triumphantly to their shoulders and paraded her around the ring before carrying her out.

Arruza looked pleased as I returned to my seat and said he could tell I had enjoyed my first taste of the ring. He invited me to return again whenever my work would allow. With such an eventful day, I looked forward to my next *tienta*.

As the months passed, I was invited to many other *tientas*.

With each new experience in the ring, I became more fascinated. Was it the challenge and danger that mesmerized me? It was more than that. To me it was a man's art, a man's sport, and only the bravest entered the ring. For me, it was a way to escape the body everyone saw. In the bullring the person inside could come out.

✳ ✳ ✳

My contract at Ciro's ended. As usual, before the last show, I was seated at Valerie Black's table. When I spoke of my next contract in Acapulco, she hinted, "I've always wanted to go there." She paused and added, "My chauffeur could drive us. We could leave early in the morning, and you'd have a whole day before you open. Would you like that?"

Always cautious, and not wanting to place myself in a position where I might end up stranded on a deserted road with her chauffeur, I said, "Sounds great, but better still, let your chauffeur stay here in Mexico City, and I'll drive the limousine to Acapulco."

"Wonderful," she smiled.

We departed early the next morning, and as the sleek limousine hummed over the narrow winding roads toward Acapulco, Valerie became more and more enthralled by the visual beauty of this romantic country. I had worked in Acapulco several times but had never driven there. After four hours on the road, we came upon a hotel named Hacienda Vista Hermosa, where we decided to stay. We were told that during the 16th century it had been the castle of Cortés, the conqueror of Mexico. The stable had been reconstructed into a nightclub with small private dining rooms that had been horse stalls hundreds of years ago, and mariachi music could be heard throughout the hotel.

I was trying desperately not to look awestruck as the bellboy, showing us to our rooms, opened the door with a 12-inch key. Once inside, he lit a fire for us. Thick black iron hinges held the massive arched door, which was hand-hewn from heavy timber. The night latch, a sliding railroad tie, added to the magical atmosphere.

I stood at the window, too busy admiring the view of the mountains to be aware of the time, when Valerie came to my room elegantly dressed for dinner.

We dined, enjoyed our surroundings, and talked. "Just listen to me," she said, "when you finish Acapulco, we'll go directly to the West Coast. I have connections."

Early the next morning we began the balance of our trip, and by late afternoon we arrived in Acapulco. Thick palms surrounded the coastal town, and every cliff cradled a sprawling hotel. The sights from the car were breathtaking as we made our way to the Las Americas Hotel.

Each room had an outside terrace, a lounge, and a bar—all very private. It was an ideally romantic, picturesque setting overlooking the Gulf of Mexico. The nightclub and dance floor were built into rock ledges. Valerie loved the sun in the afternoon and the nightclubs in the evening. After my last show each night, we made the rounds and visited every nightspot in Acapulco. Even though Valerie was about 50, she was like a teenage girl filled with enthusiasm. I secretly wished my mother could have had such a life.

One afternoon after rehearsal I found her brimming with excitement. "Look what I have for you!" she announced, waving an assortment of bundles she held in both arms. "Let's go to your room and I'll show you."

When we got to my room, she opened box after box until a wardrobe of beautiful clothes covered the bed. Along with them lay a handsome-looking gold watch.

"I bought everything in white. They'll look wonderful with your tan," she said.

"I can't accept these, Valerie."

"Why not? I want you to look this way when you take me out. Besides, June," she stepped closer to me, "I think we should get to know each other better. Guess what I want to do?" Before I could answer, she said, "I want to go swimming with you, have cocktails with you, and go to bed with you—in that order."

I stood there with mixed feelings of flattery, sadness, and much disappointment in her. I poured a drink, walked around, and mulled over the situation as she continued following me about. *Well, I'll be damned,* I thought. *I'm being manipulated. Now, we can't have that! How could I have missed it?*

I could only stare at her as her maternal look transformed into kitten-like flirtation. "How did I know, you wonder?" she said. "Darling, all the women know. The only ones you have fooled are the men. I'm very interested in your career, but there's nothing wrong with a little pleasure, now is there?"

Trying to repress any sexual thoughts, I turned to her. "All of these gifts are beautiful, but I can't accept them."

"By the way," she interjected, waving me off the subject, "I took the liberty of calling a producer, Sonny Bargolis. He's in town, and I invited him here to see your show tomorrow night."

After the show the following evening, Valerie introduced me to Mr. Bargolis, a distinguished-looking man with a dark complexion. Speaking through a thin smile, he commented, "June, Valerie knows talent when she sees it. I'm placing several calls to some influential people in California. I want to take you there and see if we can't break you into pictures."

Wonderful, I thought. *How wonderful. Almost too good to be true.*

The next evening after the show, Mr. Bargolis invited us to a party in his suite. He introduced me to 25 or more guests at the party, including Johnny Weismuller, who was in Mexico to film a Tarzan movie, and Paulette Goddard, who was once considered the most likely candidate to play Scarlett O'Hara in *Gone With the Wind* before Vivian Leigh was selected. And such a "natural" Scarlett she was. Miss Goddard, the most vivacious woman at the party, delighted in keeping the men's attention as they hurried to be the first to fill her glass and bring her food. Tarzan, on the other hand, drew the attention of all hotel guests as he climbed outside the building and swung from balcony to balcony while belting out his jungle call.

While Valerie and Sonny Bargolis were busy occupying each other's time, I watched as the lovely Miss Goddard made her way toward me. "Hi, June," she smiled. "Aren't you going to wish me a happy birthday?"

"Well, certainly," I grinned. "Happy birthday."

From there on I felt completely at a loss for words.

She spent the next hour at my side, talking about everything from the weather to my show to characters she had portrayed in the movies.

As gentlemen approached, she'd wave them off, shaking an arm adorned with tiny gold bracelets and saying, "Go away now, you cute thing. Can't you see we're talking?" And they'd walk away feeling special, having had her attention.

When she was ready to leave she took my hand and said, "After the party, come to my room, and we'll go swimming."

Of course I agreed. I told her I'd join her shortly, then walked to the bathroom, smiling all the way, feeling as flattered as the men had.

I was out of the room only a short time. When I returned, the room was quiet, and everyone was gone except Sonny Bargolis.

"Where is everyone? Where's Valerie?" I asked.

"She'll be back soon." As he walked toward me, I watched in disbelief as he removed his jacket, vest, and tie.

"Valerie wants this too, June. We thought we could..."

Pushing aside a heavy black travel bag on the dresser, he reached into his pocket and placed a beautiful amethyst bracelet and ring beside it.

"I want you to have these," he said. "I thought the three of us could..." He started to unbutton his shirt.

Mad as hell, I grabbed the heavy black bag and slammed it against his head, bringing him to his knees. Blood oozed from his scalp and dripped from his forehead to the floor. He was still kneeling as I closed the door to his suite.

Once in my room, I called a bellboy to deliver Valerie's boxes of gifts to her when she returned. I poured a drink, jumped in the shower, and after some time began to relax.

Recalling Paulette Goddard's earlier invitation, I grabbed a swimsuit and headed for her room.

"I'd just about given up on you," she said, peeking through a tiny slit as the door opened. "Come in."

Paulette stood before me wearing a white lace negligee. Flickering light radiated from 20 or more candles placed around the room. The candlelight revealed her nude body under the white lace as well as gold bracelets that went halfway up her arm. Her dark hair fell loosely to her shoulders. Seeing my surprise, she laughed and led me into the room. Then, with a playful look, she allowed the negligee to slip from her shoulders and fall softly to the floor as she said with a darling grin, "The swimming can wait."

Much later, sitting by the pool with her alone, I told Paulette about the incident that had taken place earlier that evening. She recounted a similar encounter she'd once had with a producer.

"That goes with the profession," she laughed. "You'll just have to do it. You'll see. Someday you'll just have to," and with another darling grin, she slipped into the water, swam to the bottom, and continued to the other side. From the opposite end of the pool she stirred an undercurrent in the water. After a moment she made her way underwater toward me. Then with a gush of force, her hand appeared above the surface holding her bathing suit.

My God, I thought, as I looked at her naked body in the water. *Such beauty. How could anyone think of choosing men?*

✳ ✳ ✳

When my engagement in Acapulco ended, Valerie's chauffeur arrived to pick up her bags and take her to the airport to return to Boston, and I went back to Mexico City.

In my room at the Reforma, while packing to prepare for a trip back to the States, I heard a knock at the door.

"Who's there?" I asked, but heard no answer. Thinking it must be the maid, I opened the door to reveal the back of a woman in a full-length sable coat.

"Yes? Who is it?"

As she turned around, I immediately recognized the movement. There was no mistake. It was Alta. As she walked toward me, the scent of her perfume reminded me of passionate moments on fur rugs, satin sheets, and sandy beaches. I felt the fur of her coat sleeve on the back of my neck and saw her smile. With my hands on her waist, I stepped backward, slowly, but deliberately moving away. "How did you know I was in town?"

With a devilish smile, she said, "I've got feelers everywhere!"

My eyes glued to her curvaceous legs and figure and flawless face, I laughed and said, "Yeah? I'll bet you have."

"Don't be bitter," she said. "It's my way of life." And in a femininely aggressive way, she sauntered toward me, slipping the coat from her shoulders, and added, "I was hoping we could have a little fun."

"No, Alta. Sorry."

She gave a little shrug and said, "Well, then, tell me something. I need your advice." Extending her right hand, she flashed a large diamond. "It's three and a half karats. Should I keep the ring or the coat?" There she stood, twisting her thin blade into my skin.

"I'll tell you what, Alta, why don't you put in a little overtime and keep 'em both."

I was hurting inside. It took strength to watch her leave, and I hated myself for having that strength, but I couldn't waste another minute thinking about things I couldn't change.

Six

Arthur Godfrey's Stardust Girl

Life in Mexico, for the most part, had been happy and satisfying, but I had to get on with my career in the States. It was time to leave the mariachis, bullfights, *tientas*, the good people of Mexico...and Alta. All of these would be missed. So I obtained Sheika's permits to leave the country and headed for the States.

At home, newspaper boys on street corners shouted the words "Cold War" to describe relations between Russia and the United States. Unable to read Spanish, I had missed the happenings in the rest of the world while in Mexico. During a visit at Grandma's, I listened to her translation of a letter from her cousin in Germany. She was fortunate to be in West Berlin, but she spoke sadly of her friends in the eastern part of the country still occupied by Stalin's troops. People around me were talking about the possibility of another war.

Then in June 1950, while driving to Atlanta for a club engagement, I heard on the car radio that the communist North Korean People's Army had crossed the 38th parallel and invaded South Korea. Two days later President Truman ordered U.S. Air Force and Navy troops into South Korea to avoid further invasion by the Communists. Our wardrobe mistress, Fancy, was upset over the news since she had lost her father and brother in World War II and now feared that her son would be called to serve in the Korean War. We had a new generation of 17-year-olds who had listened to first-hand stories of the heartaches of war.

For the average person back home this war was different; news of it was broadcast nightly into our living rooms. In July 1953, eight months after President Eisenhower was sworn into office, the armistice was signed and the Korean War was over.

Once again we could watch television for pleasure. But many entertainers saw it as a threat. Many of us wondered why anyone would go to a nightclub when they could see New York acts in their home. Still, I had no trouble lining up work in every town that had a floor show. In fact, my salary and savings had grown to the degree where I could provide Mom and Dad with enough money to retire. I had kept my promise. I worked theaters and clubs, and volunteered to perform at convalescent homes as well as VFW and DAV (Disabled American Veterans) hospitals, never taking a vacation.

At times, after the last show of an engagement, I'd drive all night to be in the next city in time for an afternoon rehearsal. Frequently the shortest route from one town to another was nothing more than a narrow blacktop road.

It was often frightening for me to drive alone all night, following the luminous rays of my headlights reflecting on the white center line. Sometimes the road was so desolate that I welcomed an oncoming car or a light from a farmhouse; just knowing there were others awake comforted me.

In all my thousands of miles of driving, I never had an accident, and I had just two flat tires. The first flat occurred between Washington, D.C., and Baltimore on a six-lane highway. It was all I could do to keep from being sucked under the wheels of the huge trucks that zoomed past at 75 or 80 miles an hour. That was frightening enough, but after changing a tire between Atlanta, Ga., and Mobile, Ala., on a two-lane, pitch-dark road at 2 in the morning, I made up my mind that I needed some protection.

On my way through Georgia, I bought a 25-caliber automatic handgun. I knew absolutely nothing about guns, much less the laws governing the transportation of firearms between states, so for months I carried it everywhere I went. I never expected to use it, but I felt safer just having it on the seat beside me.

In New York I ran into a dancer, Clair McKenny, with whom I had worked several times. She was a lovely, petite brunette with dazzling blue eyes and a gorgeous figure. Having much to talk about, we arranged to meet for dinner that night. She chose a French restaurant in Greenwich Village. After dinner Clair suggested we go to a little gay bar before going home. She was quite comfortable in the bar, and I was surprised at her instant acceptance of the couples. She was definitely interested in me—it was obvious. When I suggested having a drink in my room, she nodded and said, "I thought you'd never ask."

Over drinks in my room, I noticed she was looking at the handgun on the dresser. I kept it there unless I knew the maid would be coming to make up the room. Seeing the look on Clair's face, I shrugged and explained, "It's nothing. It's not even loaded." I know I should have been more careful about leaving it in plain view, but my intentions were so innocent that I thought nothing of it. Clair didn't notice the gun for long, though, since she had just one thing on her mind. Likewise, I was lonely, and Clair was beautiful. It was obvious I wasn't the first person to hop into bed with her, and I knew I wouldn't be the last. She was seductive and playful, she was asking, and I enjoyed her to the fullest.

The next morning we had breakfast and chatted, and then she left. During the day I made my usual business phone calls. By late evening I had bathed and was ready for bed when the phone rang.

It was a man's voice. At first I thought it was an agent returning my call. "Miss Walls?" he said.

"Speaking."

"Is this June Walls?"

"Yes. Who's this?"

"Never mind that. I understand you went to bed with my girlfriend last night."

"Your girlfriend?"

"Yes. Clair McKenny."

Shocked into silence, I waited, then demanded, "Who are you?"

"I'll tell you what I want: I'm going to come to your room and pick up $500 in small bills in an hour."

My initial shock turned into fury. "You've gotta be crazy, fella!" I blurted. "What makes you think I'd give it to you?"

"I know you'll give it to me," he said. "I'll be over in an hour."

"Now, wait a minute, whoever you are—"

"No, Miss Walls, there are no minutes to wait. Five hundred in small bills or I'll call the police and tell 'em where they can find a queer who transported a gun into New York City."

Oh, God, I thought, *here we go again.* "Is Clair with you?" I asked.

"That's not important."

I felt the cage closing me in, and I had to decide instantly how to get around it. I had been sidestepping unsavory bastards everywhere, and I was certain $500 would only be the beginning. Figuring I might as well meet him head-on, I said, "Go ahead, you son of a bitch, call the police. By the way, she sure was good. Too bad you don't have enough to keep her satisfied!" And I slammed the phone down.

In 10 minutes I heard a knock at the door. "Open up! Police!" I opened the door to two plainclothes detectives, badges flashing, who walked passed me into the room.

Detective Schwartz, tall and thin, shifted his belt on his hips as Detective Johnson, blond and 30ish, looked around. I sat on the edge of the bed and watched the two of them quickly shift their eyes throughout the room.

"We've had a report," Schwartz said, "that you have a gun in here."

"Yes, I do," I said, pointing. "See it laying on the dresser?"

Johnson picked up the unloaded gun and asked me the usual name, age, and address questions, then asked how long I'd been in the city and what I was doing in New York with a gun.

"I was afraid on the road alone," I explained.

Schwartz fumbled through my gowns hanging in the closet.

"I travel all the time. Call AGVA. They'll tell you I'm a member in good standing."

"That won't be necessary. But," Johnson stared hard at me, "who's this guy who reported you?"

"I don't know him personally. He's a friend of a friend of mine."

"Friend? He called you everything in the book. He said you were a dangerous person and shouldn't be on the loose. You don't look dangerous to me. You got any idea why he would report you?"

I knew they were going to get to that, and I've never been good at lying. So, looking as wholesome as possible in my flannel pajamas and ponytail, I answered him. "He's mad because I spent last night with his girlfriend, and he was trying to blackmail me for $500. You really should be chasing *him*. I wasn't doing anything. I was just having a good time."

The two detectives looked at each other as I continued. "When I refused to pay him, he said he'd call you. I decided to take my lumps, right now."

"He sure was hot when he called in," Johnson said. "Sounded like some kind of kook. What did you say to make him so mad?"

"I said, 'Too bad you don't have enough to keep her satisfied.' And that made him mad."

Trying hard to stifle a laugh, they went into the hall and

returned after a few minutes. "Now, you know, Miss Walls," Schwartz said, "we could take you down to the station house since it's against the law to transport firearms into the state of New York. On the other hand, we could just take the gun and forget it. Now, which do you want us to do?"

"Please, officer, take the gun."

They turned toward the door, and Johnson said, "Next time be careful what kind of women you get mixed up with."

"Yes, sir," I said, still sitting on the edge of my bed. "Thanks."

When they left, I sighed in relief, feeling good about having met a couple of nice guys.

* * *

After a few days of making contacts, I left New York for Pennsylvania. My life had changed in many ways while I was in Mexico; the biggest void was feeling like I didn't belong anywhere.

The short, sometimes memorable romances I had after losing Diana were frivolous in comparison. I searched for deep, long-lasting companionship but found none. I was 30 years old and wanted to find someone I could love, someone who would love me just as much in return. That would be a gift from God, and I prayed each night for it.

Following the sale of my house in Atlanta, I purchased a home a mile from my parents in Pittsburgh. Soon after, I received a call from Morry Fremont, an agent who had followed my career for a number of years. Morry, a short, round, quiet man, was always chewing on a toothpick. I'd met him while working a club date at the William Penn Hotel.

Morry offered to keep me working constantly. I welcomed the thought, as I'd been booking myself since Bobby's disappearance. Morry's son Al, a good-looking guy my age, had his own band. He was also an excellent arranger and conductor. Al began rearranging my music, and when he was finished, it was fabulous. He was a singer's musician, and we blended well.

Morry was just what I needed, but he kept complaining about my name. He simply didn't like it. "It doesn't have the right zing," he told me. "It's too soft. We gotta change it."

"That's fine, Morry. Change it to whatever you want, but please keep the initials, because everything I've got is monogrammed. OK?"

"OK," he nodded, picking at his front tooth.

"Let's see, Jane...nah, too soft," he said, still nodding and working the pick back and forth. "Jackie, Jan..."

"That's not bad, Morry. Jan would be OK."

"OK. Jan Welch, Welks, Welles," he said. "How about Jan Welles?"

"If that's how you see it, it's OK with me," I smiled. "I could live with that." With a quick, unimposing nod from Morry, it was confirmed.

"And your next move should be television and records," he said.

"Terrific idea, Morry. I've written lyrics before. I'll write something, and Al can work up an arrangement for the tune."

"OK, Jan, it's a deal. You write the song, I'll pay for the recording session, and then I'll have a master to sell to a record company."

That evening, alone in my room, I thought of the first time I'd seen Diana in Key West. I recalled the comfort we'd found in each other. Then I remembered the last time I held her as we said goodbye, and I began to write:

> *Please don't go,*
> *Don't leave me standing here.*
> *Please don't go,*
> *Don't let me lose you, dear.*
>
> *Here's a heart that's bound to break*
> *Here's a heart that's yours to take.*

Please don't go.
Do what you will with me.
Don't you know you are my destiny?

My poor heart cries out to you.
I can't go on, I beg you.
Please don't go.

The next day, judging from Al and Morry's expressions and the twitching of Morry's toothpick, they loved it. Al began working on the arrangement immediately.

Soon we were en route to New York and the best recording facilities in the world. With an 18-piece band made up of some of the finest musicians in New York, including Billy Butterfield, I put everything I could into that song.

I went back to Pittsburgh to perform, and my reviews were very complimentary. A critic for *Billboard* wrote:

> There is something exciting happening this week at this plush Pittsburgh nitery. Perched on a piano, beautiful Jan Welles dressed up a 20-minute songalog with all the fervor and dramatic approach now being used by top wax artists. Using a hand mike with a rhinestone cord, Miss Welles sparkled thru her turn and left the audience limp when she went off with a drama-packed version of "I'll Be Seeing You."

Al showed me the review the same day we received word that Morry had sold my recording to RKO Unique Records. We were to work with Unique's Artist and Repertoire man, Joe Leahy. He had some fine voice and arrangement ideas, and we recorded three additional songs: "Kiss Me Every Time You Call Me Darling," "I'd Love to Be Wrong," and "I'm at a Dangerous Age." Joe wanted to have the follow-up releases ready to put out at the right time.

Morry, working daily to get exposure for me, received a call from from *The Arthur Godfrey Talent Scouts Show* in New York. To make it on the program, a performer had to pass five or six auditions before getting to Mr. Godfrey, who had the final say. Performers were called the day before a scheduled audition, so we had to stay in New York for six weeks, waiting beside a phone at all times. Living in the city for that long was expensive, so I had to make enough money as a featured entertainer on one club date a week to pay for food, lodging, a garage for the car, and Morry's commission.

The money I'd saved was set aside for the mortgage on my home in Pittsburgh, as well as Mom and Dad's retirement. I assured my parents on my trip home in December 1955 that I wouldn't touch my savings while waiting for the Godfrey people to call.

Morry only booked me into the best clubs, and for most of my six-week stay in New York, I played one night each weekend at Grossinger's. A $100 club date would cover expenses with some left over for the unexpected. At this salary, my reputation and income remained high. Morry could have kept me working for less money, but once an entertainer works a cheap venue, the better clubs won't touch them. Every act has an image; if they lower it, they're branded for the rest of their career.

Morry and I had found two inexpensive, clean hotel rooms for $7 a week, plus $5 a week for parking. My 6-by-8 room had no phone, and to have ample walking space I had to keep my luggage under the single bed. The room had a wash basin, a coat hook, and a 25-watt light bulb hanging from the ceiling. If I wanted to read, I had to go to the lobby.

We put in many hours there, waiting. Our daily guard duty by the pay phone was mandatory. If we both had to go out at the same time, we talked the desk clerk into taking a message.

I decided I could eat at a local diner on $1 a day, which would bring my weekly expenses after Morry's commission to $15. Needick's was a little hole in the wall with no tables, only stools and a counter, that served eggs, bacon, toast, orange juice, and coffee for a buck. I lost weight, which was fine for a while, but I was constantly hungry.

My first audition for *The Godfrey Show* went smoothly, so I celebrated with an extra meal at Needick's. In due course, I passed the second audition. More waiting, more hunger. Then two more successful auditions—four total. Days passed into weeks. Time dragged as Morry and I took turns waiting for another call. We knew we were getting close and didn't dare leave the phone unattended for a moment.

Morry was sitting in the phone booth when the call came. He chewed his toothpick and listened, said a few words, and hung up. Then he turned to me with a big smile. "You made it! You've got an audition with 'The Old Redhead,' Godfrey himself!"

That's when the nervousness started. After I decided on a song, every note, every gesture ran through my mind continuously. I had a serious case of the jitters. This was the most important audition in my life so far; it just had to go well. Anything less was unthinkable. But the busier I kept myself, the more quickly time passed.

Standing in the CBS audition room with Mr. Godfrey and his assistants, I felt as though all my studying, showmanship, and even mistakes—everything I had ever done—had prepared me for this moment. All the breathing exercises, planning, hard knocks, and tears had led to this crucial test of my talent. Suddenly Mr. Godfrey broke the silence. "What are you going to sing, Jan?"

Of all the songs ever written, none was more fitting than the one I'd chosen. "Mr. Godfrey," I said, "I'd like to sing 'Living the Life I Love.'" The accompanist gave me an arpeggio, and for a second I closed my eyes and focused on giving my finest performance yet. I'd come a long way from the cobblestone streets on the bread route, and I was grateful for this. Recalling all the early years, I began to sing. At the end, the lyrics were like my evening prayer: "And when I lay me down to sleep / If I just wake up in the morning,

I'm thankful / In my heart I keep my treasures stored, thank the Lord / I'm living...I'm living the life I love."

When I finished, I held my breath and was aware of total silence. I was immobile. At last Mr. Godfrey said, "Jan, that was just beautiful." Then he immediately turned and left.

Could he turn me down now? I wondered. *Surely not.*

As the days passed, the wait in the lobby was almost more than Morry and I could bear. Finally, the pay phone rang. Morry took the call, his toothpick twitched, and I heard him say, "OK." He hung up the receiver and turned to me. "You made it! Your big chance comes January 16."

We had one week to prepare for the live Monday night show. It was really important to select the right song, and I couldn't help wondering who I'd be competing against.

I spent most of the next week practicing. Working diligently and having little money, I was becoming thin as a rail.

The day before the show, I choked a little when Morry said, "The first thing we're going to do today is move to a better hotel. If you win tomorrow night, you can't be seen going in and out of this place."

Even though I was shocked at the suggestion, Morry convinced me, and I packed my bags and moved to the President Hotel. It wasn't the biggest hotel in town, but the address was respectable. After we moved my car to a more expensive parking lot, all I had in my pocket was three pennies and a paper clip.

I was relaxing in my room when a delicious aroma, like broiled steak, wafted in. *Probably room service for the more affluent guests,* I thought. Several minutes later I found myself searching the pockets of my clothing and bags for any loose change I might have overlooked. Then I remembered I had already done this in the parking lot.

I decided to take a walk to get away from the mouth-watering aroma. It was cold, so I wrapped a coat tightly around me and hurried outside. But I couldn't escape: I saw reminders of food all around me. A sign in a window advertised the special of the day: hot buttered vegetables.

When I was a kid, Mom, Dad, and I would go down to the wharf on the Ohio River every week with the Williamses to buy fresh vegetables. Mama rarely had meat on the table, since it was expensive, but she always cooked fresh vegetables. Sometimes we'd buy a bushel basket of green beans, peas, or corn, and she and Mrs. Williams would can them for the winter. As it turned dark on the wharf, we'd go to the fires glowing in metal drums and buy roasted ears of corn. Being poor didn't matter when we could stand in the warmth with our neighbors, husk an ear of corn, and dip it into a pan of melted butter. Looking over my ear of corn, I'd see flames dancing in the eyes of all the friendly folks gathered there.

Standing outside the restaurant on that cold day, I could still taste the flavor of that corn. I had to win on *The Godfrey Show* if it took every fiber in my body, but I couldn't win on an empty stomach. Wrapping my coat tighter around me, I came upon a small grill on 8th Avenue. The windows were steamy from the simmering pots of food. Pangs in my stomach pulled me to a vacant stool at the back of the diner.

A friendly Italian man took my order for roast beef with gravy, mashed potatoes, vegetables, and milk. My plate was heaping. I ate slowly, savoring every bite. When I finished I asked the man behind the counter if he was the owner. "Yes, I'm Joe Romani," he told me.

"I'm broke," I said. "I'm so sorry to tell you this, but I was hungry. Can I wash dishes for you? Clean for you? Anything?"

There were other people in the grill, two men and a woman at the counter. I felt myself blush in shame, and added quickly, "I'll pay you back, really I will." Looking around wildly, trying to convince him, I said, "I'm on *The Arthur Godfrey Talent Scouts Show* tomorrow night, and I'll pay you back. I promise. Win or lose, I'll pay you back."

"Sure, sure," he mumbled. I could tell this wasn't the

first time he'd been clipped. "Forget it," he said. "Just forget it." He waved me off in disgust.

All through my apology, I kept asking him to watch the show the next night. He would see me win, and then I'd come back and pay him for the meal.

Back in my room I fell asleep, content as a baby. After an hour or so, Morry knocked on the door and walked in with a big smile. Still, I could tell he was anxious about something.

He told me he knew I was under a lot of pressure and that I didn't have any close friends. "Ya gotta find time to meet someone for a drink and relax," he'd often tell me.

He was straight, but he wanted me to have companionship and didn't quite know what to do for me. So, with his hat cocked on the side of his head and his toothpick in his mouth, he said, "Since it's taken us so long to get this far and we've worked so hard, is there any last-minute thing you'd like? Maybe I could buy you a drink or something? What would make you happy?"

I jumped at the offer. "Morry," I said, "I'm so damn tired of working in straight clubs and having your lifestyle shoved down my throat. Hell, yes! I'd like to just sit in a gay bar and have a couple of drinks with you and feel comfortable for a change, with my people. Would you do that for me?"

"Sure, I would, Jan. We could go to Greenwich Village," Morry smiled.

"Would you? I could relax there, Morry, like nowhere else. I haven't seen a gay person for months. I'm beginning to think there aren't any."

He chuckled a bit and asked, "Will I be safe?"

"Oh, Morry, I won't let any of those guys get you. I'll protect you," I joked.

"OK, let's have a good time. This one's on me!" Little 5-foot-4 Morry looked about 10 feet tall right then.

We hopped a subway, hurried to Greenwich Village, and walked until I saw what I was sure was a gay bar.

"You know, this is a new experience for me," Morry said, with his eyebrows raised and chin tucked.

"Cheer up, Morry. You'll be all right."

His expression was priceless, like he was bringing a big bag jelly beans into a room full of hungry kids.

The bar seemed like a friendly place, so we climbed onto the closest barstools, and I took a deep sigh of relief. I could actually feel my breathing slow to a calm rhythm. There were couples—fellows together, girls together—and I felt at home. When I was growing up, there were no such clubs. As far as I knew, there were no such people. Like many others, I thought I was the only one, but 14 years had made a big difference. These people weren't hiding. They weren't ashamed. They were proud, decent people. There were all types, some in business suits and some who appeared a bit more unconventional. I was having fun just being there.

Turning slightly toward me, Morry asked seriously, "Do I look funny in here? How will they know I'm not—"

"They won't, Morry."

His eyebrows started to twitch, and his toothpick rattled from side to side. A clean-cut, good-looking gentleman was sitting at the end of the bar. He glanced our way several times, and I knew he wasn't looking at me. Boy, was that a good feeling for a change. Just for the hell of it, trying to have fun, I said to Morry, "Hey, see that guy at the end of the bar? I think he likes the way you look. He hasn't looked anywhere else since you sat down, and I know he's not looking at me."

"Come on, Jan."

"No, honest. He probably knows a nice guy when he sees one."

The toothpick twittled to the other side of Morry's mouth. "What do I do if he comes over and says hello?"

"The same thing you'd do if he wasn't gay—say hello."

Looking around, giving Morry a breather, I saw the meaningful expressions on the faces around me, and I deeply felt they were my people. I was at home.

On the way back to the hotel, I thanked Morry and asked him how he liked the experience.

"Wasn't bad at all. In fact, everyone was friendly. They seem like good people."

"We're all good people, and you're good people too, Morry, and I'm gonna win for you tomorrow night."

In my room that night I lay in bed running through the events of the last few hours. Morry would never know how much that evening meant to me. It reaffirmed that I belonged somewhere. Then my thoughts turned to the man at the grill. I felt sad that I had stooped so low, but at least I wasn't hungry.

As I stared up at the dark ceiling, I repeated to myself, "I've gotta win, I've gotta win" over and over until at last sleep took over.

✳ ✳ ✳

For the past six weeks my mother had been forwarding my mail to a P.O. box in New York. The day after the Godfrey people had called, I received a letter from a friend who had been trying to locate me. "I'm sure you've heard by now that Diana has a little girl," she wrote.

I hadn't heard. Silently I wished Diana well, but I was thankful that my rehearsals for *The Godfrey Show* were long and arduous; it kept my mind off the news.

My song, "No Arms Can Ever Hold You," was close to perfect, but so were the other acts—a piano duet and a singing quartet from Brooklyn. The duet was superb, and I knew I couldn't expect to walk all over the quartet either.

Before the show, a cathedral hush filled my dressing room as I sipped my drink. It was no different from waiting to do any other show. No flowers, no phone calls, no telegrams, no visitors. Just me. Then suddenly I heard a bang on the door, and someone announced, "Three minutes to show time."

I busied myself with small details, making certain my hair, gown, and makeup looked perfect. Finally, the minutes slipped by, and I heard, "Shooooow time!"

The duet went first and must have been well received, since the house filled with applause.

In a flat across town, the owner of the grill, Joe Romani, and his wife reluctantly sat before a 19-inch black-and-white TV to watch the talent show. They were both angry over having been taken again, yet Joe was hopeful. Perhaps, just perhaps, the redhead hadn't lied. Then the two of them heard Mr. Godfrey announce, "Jan Welles." The musical introduction started, and with his eyes fixed steadily on the set Joe said, "That's her! That's the girl!"

"Really, Joe? You sure?"

Instantly his outstretched arms placed a sudden hush on the living room.

For me, everything seemed to be coming together. I thought of every little club and theater I'd worked in over the years. I remembered all the hard work, the heartaches, and the disappointments. And then the orchestra played the introduction, I recalled an image of a lovely woman in pink ankle-straps and a pink halter dress descending a flight of stairs in Key West, and I began to sing: "No arms could ever hold you / Like these arms of mine..."

The song was beautiful, and I sang it with all I had. I was elated. And the audience sensed it; they were with me to the last note. Their applause was overwhelming. Lelia Wilson Smith, Jane Froman, and Billie Holiday had all been good teachers.

The last act went on, but I was so busy questioning my performance that the quartet finished before I knew it. Then each contestant came back onstage to repeat a line or two from their performance while the audience cast its vote on the applause meter. I couldn't see the meter or consciously register the applause. I seemed to be moving in a mechanical state until I heard Mr. Godfrey say, "I guess there's no doubt who the winner is." For a moment I was oblivious to everything. Then I felt Morry's hand on my shoulder pushing me out onstage. "Go get it, Jan!" he said. "You won!"

Never had I expected such a response. I had worked for it, prepared for it, but couldn't believe I made it, and my God, was I grateful. I bowed with deep appreciation. Coming up from my bow, I paused and listened to all that sound and I thought, *Look! You're accepting me, a lesbian. Your applause is for all the members of my club.* And with that, the shocking release came.

As tears streamed down my face, Mr. Godfrey reached for his handkerchief. "Here it is, Jan. Go ahead and weep," he smiled. Turning to the audience, he made a remark that would stick with me throughout my career: "I see some stardust 'round here, don't you?" Applause erupted throughout the house. Instantly I became Arthur Godfrey's "Stardust Girl That Cried." But I was the only one who knew the real reason for the tears.

I have no memory of how I got through the crowd and back to the dressing room. One moment you're no one in particular and the next you're somebody. The change was unbelievable. Everybody wanted to offer congratulations. They were all so cheerful, such fine people.

I asked to have a moment alone in my dressing room, but Morry's banging on the door brought me back to earth.

"You were electric, Jan. The night belongs to you!" He hugged me and through tears reaffirmed his belief in me. Then sanity returned as he said, "Let's eat."

"Boy, could I go for that. But not Needick's, Morry, please."

"Right! Let's splurge. We'll go to Horn & Hardart's."

That's like going from White Castle to McDonald's.

I changed quickly, and we headed for the elevator. When the elevator doors opened into the CBS lobby, we saw people filling the entire vestibule. It was unlike anything I had ever experienced. Each person had paper and pencil in hand and offered congratulations. I signed autographs all the way to the cab and even for the cab driver.

Word spread fast. A crowd was waiting at the President Hotel when we returned from dinner. I signed more autographs all through the lobby, in the elevator, and up to my room. When the door closed, I heard the telephone ringing. (Yes, there was a phone in the new room!) One call after another came, from people all over the country; most were strangers, friendly people wishing me well. And the phone rang all night.

The next day I was back at CBS at 7 A.M. for makeup, rehearsal, and the morning show. That's when Mr. Godfrey announced his plans to keep me on a show each morning, Monday through Friday, with Pat Boone and Miyoshi Umeki, the singer and actress who later went on to win a Best Supporting Actress Oscar in 1957 for her role in *Sayonara*.

After the morning show I remembered my most important errand of the day: going back to the grill on 8th Avenue. I took a cab to the diner and asked the driver to wait. When I walked through the door, Mr. Romani and his wife let out a loud shriek and came from behind the counter, throwing their hands in the air and then around me. "You won!" they shouted. Joe Romani's eyes glistened with tears.

Never could I repay him or thank him enough for what he had done for me. I gave him a 20 and an autograph, and I wondered if I could have sung as confidently on an empty stomach.

When I returned to my hotel room around 6 o'clock, the phone was ringing, and it continued until late in the evening. The telegrams and flowers poured in, some from friends like Jody Barns, Mingo, and Betty and Florence, some from people I had known along the way, and many from people I'd never met.

On one call, a voice said, "Hi, is this that sexy-looking redhead who sings the hell out of a song?" It was Penny Westman, calling to congratulate me.

And then it came, the call I'd been waiting for but thought I'd never receive. An unforgettable honey-dripping voice said, "June?"

"Yes."

"Congratulations, sweetheart! I'm so proud of you."

"Diana?" I said, collapsing into a chair. I couldn't believe it. It had been 12 years.

"Is it really you?" I said, catching myself sounding too happy.

Diana sounded just the same. There were a hundred questions to ask. We talked about the good times we'd had, working and playing together, and about my new name, which she said she liked. Finally, after some time, she offered information about herself and the events that had transpired since I'd last seen her.

She told me she had married in 1947. "Truth be known," she said, "I got married to keep my family off my back. I did it out of spite. Isn't that a laugh? My marriage lasted six months, then Greg and I separated. We were divorced in '49. I have a daughter, Jami, but I had to fight like hell for custody of her."

"You're not dancing anymore?" I asked.

"I quit show business. I'm not doing anything now."

I felt like I was on cloud nine. "I'd love to see you, Diana. I'll be at this hotel for a few weeks. Why don't you come to New York? We could spend some time together." I had missed her terribly and wanted to tell her but couldn't allow myself to become that vulnerable. I'd been disappointed too many times.

Hearing her excitement, I said, "Please try to make it. Just give me a call when your plans are set."

God, she sounded great. Everything was happening so fast it was hard to find time for my own private moments.

The next morning, after the show, the CBS mail clerk delivered boxes filled with fan mail. When you're unaccustomed to fame, you lose all notion of what is reasonable. I certainly wasn't prepared for this. Every day cardboard boxes filled with fan letters were delivered to me by cab, and soon they filled my hotel room. Morry and I looked at each other in desperation.

The first week one of the fans started a club with official membership cards and Jan Welles pins. Many times that week I'd sit in the stillness of my room and think what a change one show had made. If I hadn't worked so damn hard to get this far, I'd have sworn it was a mistake. As the boxes of mail arrived, I read words of praise from strangers, but I knew they hadn't accepted the real me. I read every letter with that in mind.

Morry hired York Hall Associates to handle publicity. They had a strong track record, and we needed professionals to take charge of that department. We were introduced to Stanley Baker, a quick-thinking fast-talker who enjoyed handling several things at once.

At a meeting in his office, he asked, "What's your hobby, Jan? We gotta come up with something spectacular, like skydiving or something—something to boost the momentum of your career." Looking wide-eyed, he pressed his face between his hands, making a V of wrinkles under his eyes.

"What about waterskiing or deep-sea diving?" he asked. "Did you ever do anything like that while you were in Mexico?"

"On Sundays I went to the bullfights, and I often went to *tientas*," I said. "That's where breeders test their heifers for bravery. I tested a few, and they said I was pretty good."

Stanley rummaged through the clutter on his desk, looking for something. After a few minutes he said, "Let me think on this. I'll give you a call in a day or two."

Thinking no more of the conversation, I went back to CBS and was looking through my music in preparation for the Wednesday night *Godfrey and His Friends* show when Mr. Godfrey called me into his office to discuss a number.

He was a rather relaxed man who spoke in a way that put one immediately at ease. "Jan," he said, "I want ya to sing 'Love Is a Many Splendored Thing.' It's a pretty tune, and I'd like ya to do it in a garden scene with flowers. Lotsa flowers and a choir and orchestra and violins, a big string section. How's that sound?"

"It sounds like quite a production, Mr. Godfrey."

"Good, that's what it's gonna be. I'm gonna call Best and Company to come over and fit ya for a special gown with a big net skirt, like a Cinderella type. You'd like that, wouldn't ya?"

"Yes," I gulped. "Sounds beautiful."

As I was leaving, I heard him call the wardrobe department to make the fitting arrangements.

The next morning I met with Morry in the CBS green room and told him about the production number Mr. Godfrey was planning for the Wednesday night show.

"Sounds fantastic," Morry said.

"Morry, flowers? A garden? Cinderella?" I sat there in a funk. "That's not me. They're getting further away from me all the time."

"Right," he said laughing, "but they're still not ready for you in a tux."

The next day Best and Company sent a frilly ice-blue gown for my number—certainly the most feminine thing I'd ever had to wear.

Thursday morning after the show, Mr. Godfrey called me into his office again. "Jan," he said, "that production number was your signature. From here on, 'Love Is a Many Splendored Thing' should be your theme song. Look at these reviews." He picked up a handful of clippings. "And they tell me the phone calls have been coming in all morning with raves about you and 'Splendored Thing.' Now, how'd ya like to go to Miami this weekend for a show at the Kenilworth Hotel and follow up with two weeks at the Vagabond Club?"

"Of course!" I said, jumping at the chance, which brought a jolly laugh from Mr. Godfrey.

"It'll be an hour-long show for $1,500, Jan. And at the Vagabond Club, you'll do a 20-minute spot each night for $950 a week."

Thanking him, I said, "Wonderful, Mr. Godfrey!" I was to leave the following Saturday morning.

* * *

Everything positive was happening at once, but I had no one with whom to share my happiness except Morry. It had been two weeks since Diana's call, and she was constantly on my mind.

Arriving in the pink-and-white world of Miami Beach, I saw newspapers filled with ads for *The Jan Welles Show*. After checking in at the Kenilworth, I went to rehearsal and then to my room to rest before the performance that evening.

As the sky darkened, I turned out the lights, fixed a drink, and sat at the window watching the shiny, expensive cars pull into the circle drive below. They discharged elegantly dressed couples who were coming to see my show. I wondered if they could be some of the fine people who hadn't even noticed my bloody shoes in the street. Clenching my fist in victory, I couldn't wait to sing to them. I kept thinking, *You're coming to see me, a lesbian.* I wanted so much to be honest with them. For years I'd been singing all sorts of songs written for men to sing to women, such as "She's Funny That Way," "Chloe," and "You Are Too Beautiful." The audience would just smile and applaud, the lesbian subtext clearly going over their heads. Perhaps more than anything I wanted to test them and see if they could be as honest with me as I was with them. Then perhaps they'd say, "We like you anyway" as they stood to applaud.

Even though I felt phony putting on a feminine net gown, 16 years in show business teaches one self-control. If I hid my feelings each night, no one would know I was in there.

The phone rang just as I was almost finished getting ready, and I heard, "We're ready for you, Miss Welles." It was the manager.

Before I left my room, I always made a last-minute check

in front of a mirror to see if I looked feminine enough to give the audience what they wanted. So I checked the mirror and asked myself, "One rhinestone bracelet? Nah. It's girlier with two. Drop earrings? OK, they'll like this. Will they like *me*? Nah, they'd never like me, so I'll have to cover myself up. I'll cover myself up with furs, rhinestones, slinky gowns, and four-inch heels, and maybe, just maybe, they'll like what they see." I gave myself a secret wink in the mirror.

I opened the door and stepped awkwardly into the hall, hoping I wouldn't meet anyone. If anyone said hello, I'd probably say, "How the hell are ya?" and blow my cover.

I reached the elevator. Empty. Terrific. One more moment alone. Third floor. Second floor. First floor. The doors opened to dozens of smiling faces waiting for me to fulfill their dreams of what they thought I was. Stepping from the elevator, I smelled expensive perfume everywhere. The graciousness of each touch and remark was gratifying. I had waited so long for this, but I could only smile and nod.

I wondered where they'd been keeping themselves for the past 16 years. The men were handsomely dressed in evening clothes, and the women were wearing jewels and expensive furs, but I was the same as always. As I made my way through the lobby, through the dining room, and to the mike, the applause started and continued for a long time, and I hadn't even opened my mouth.

The hour sped by, but it seemed I had been singing only a few minutes; they were so responsive.

After that engagement, for the next two weeks I worked the Vagabond Club, which was owned by a singing group who had also won on *Arthur Godfrey's Talent Scouts*. They had many hit records, including the popular "No, Not Much." They were wonderful to work for, and the club was packed nightly.

At a rehearsal the second week, one of the owners came over to where I was sorting out my music for the band and flashed a copy of *This Week* magazine in front of me. "Check out page 4," he said.

Before I could oblige, he pulled the magazine from my view and said, "Listen to this, Jan: 'Everyone loves a winner, and there's never been a lovelier winner than Jan Welles, the singer who recently was tagged the Stardust Girl by Arthur Godfrey, now a hold-over at the Vagabond Club.

" 'Since her arrival in town—a couple of weeks ago—Jan has been the subject of every columnist, critic, talent scout, booking agent, and fan. The Pittsburgh lass—who's been shrouded in anonymity for a decade—is like a butterfly that just emerged from a cocoon. She's flying high, but the new wings seem strange. She's as dazzled as a Cinderella transformed into a royal princess!' Etcetera, etcetera...and listen to this:

" 'She can hold the final notes of a ballad longer than anyone we've ever listened to. She literally has you gasping as you sit on the edge of your seat. "No Arms Can Ever Hold You" is the ditty that catapulted her to nationwide recognition. It should be her permanent theme song.' "

After closing at the Vagabond Club, I returned to New York. Shortly after arriving at the hotel, I received a call from Diana, who told me she'd be in town in a week and could stay for two months. I could hardly believe my ears. We made arrangements to meet at the airport cocktail lounge.

Hearing of Diana's plans, I rushed out and rented a furnished apartment in Forest Hills, Queens, and looked forward to our living like other couples, if only for a short while.

Between getting the apartment ready and working each morning on Godfrey's morning show, the week passed quickly. My heart pounded as I sat in the airport cocktail lounge in plain view of the door. Diana walked in looking even lovelier than I had remembered.

She spotted me from across the room. Slowly I rose from the chair, unsure of her reaction. She stepped quickly toward me. In one swift move we grabbed each other and held on tightly. There was no kiss; it wouldn't have been accepted in public. After waiting 12 years for this moment, just being together was all that mattered.

Seven

¡Torera!

The years had been more than complimentary to Diana. Maturity had crept in, and she wore it well. The same warmth and attraction I had known before was still there, almost as though there had been no lapse of time. And that utterly charming face had become even more charming over the years.

Diana's daughter, Jami, who was 11, would be with staying with her grandmother for the two-month visit. After that, she would be with her father for six weeks.

Diana joined me at my table. We chatted, and after a while she said, "There are so many questions, so much to tell."

Raising my glass, I said, "For the moment, let's start with now and go forward. OK?"

I had almost forgotten I had an appointment in an hour with Morry at Stanley's office. Diana understood, familiar with the rat race of show business. We hurried through our drinks and left.

As Diana and I entered the office, Stanley was explaining something to Morry. "Yeah, that's right!" he said. "And it's never been done before." He walked to the front of his desk and sat on the edge.

Stanley saw us, nodded, and gestured toward two chairs.

Once we were seated, he continued, "Jan, how would you like to be a bullfighter?"

The words shocked even me. "You're serious?"

"The International Bullfighting Fair is in the Dominican Republic this year," Stanley said. "They'd like to have about 500,000 people in attendance. President Trujillo, on the advice of the director of publicity for the Fair, has decided to stage a grand spectacle featuring an American. They've never had a bullfight down there, and it would be a bloodless fight." Looking directly at me, he explained, "So you wouldn't have to kill the bull, Jan. Anyhow, they're looking for an American to do it in order to draw in American tourists."

I was speechless.

"Morry, her career can't ride on the Godfrey win forever," Stanley went on. "We have to find a catalyst to take her the rest of the way, something out of the ordinary. Bullfighting would do it. Jan, if you could learn the basics, think a minute—an American singer *and* bullfighter!"

The four of us sat in silence. Morry nervously rolled a toothpick between his teeth, and I visualized myself in the suit of lights.

Looking at the three of them, I caught Diana's worried look. "What do you think?" I asked.

"Jan, it's your decision," she said. "But God, it would be dangerous."

I knew bullfighting was the highest-paid profession per minute in the world, but I was thinking more of the art and the power I had felt in the ring. Still, I was dubious. Stanley kept his intense glare on me, and Morry fixed his eyes on Stanley.

They knew the business, so if this was what they thought my career needed, I had to trust them. I turned to Diana and asked, "Would you go with me?"

"I'd have to arrange a trip home before we left the country," she said. "But yes, I'd love to go with you."

That was all I needed. "OK, I'll do it, but only if Carlos Arruza will teach me."

"Just imagine, Jan," Morry said, "Stanley will get you the cover of *Life* magazine, and we'll tie your singing, records, *The Godfrey Show,* and bullfighting all together." He was brimming with excitement.

Stanley started making calls, first to directors to stage the event and then to renowned matador Carlos Arruza at his ranch in Mexico.

Meanwhile, Stanley called Joe Leahy, the A&R man at RKO Unique Records, and explained what we were planning with the bullfight. Joe said he would work up an LP called *Torera* and have it ready to cut when I got back from the fight at the Fair.

Diana was so excited about the trip to both Mexico and the Dominican Republic. We left the office, grabbed a bite to eat, and returned to the apartment just as the phone was ringing. It was Stanley.

"Jan, Carlos Arruza called, saying he'd do it if you're willing to put in two months of hard work. It would take that long, he said, to learn enough to even think about the first fight. Carlos said you could use a guest room in his home until you can find a place of your own."

As he was talking, I paced back and forth, wondering if I was making the right decision. I looked at Diana and thought, *We could have it all now. She's all I really want,* and I heard Stanley say, "This'll do it for us, Jan."

Everyone was depending on me, and I couldn't let them down. "OK, Stan, that's great," I said. "I'll talk to you later."

I hung up the phone and looked at Diana. We were finally alone. Our long-awaited evening together had arrived.

Soft strains of a concerto filled the bedroom, which was aglow with candlelight and embers of a slow-burning fire. Her skin felt like fine velvet, and the emotion we felt for each other was overpowering. As the evening passed, we were aware only of each other, and the vast world outside held little meaning.

The candlewicks sputtered in floating wax and the wood in the fire had long turned to ash as I held her late into the night. And then the morning came, spreading sunlight across the bed. Watching Diana sleep, I wondered if she knew how special and loved she made me feel.

Later that morning we learned that the plans for the trip had been confirmed. Now, with Diana by my side, I worried about nothing and was happy about everything. I made up my mind to go forth with determination for success.

We spent the following week taking care of last-minute details. Everything was packed when Stanley called and said he had a contract for me at the Hotel Jaragua in Ciudad Trujillo for two weeks right before the bullfight.

"They remembered the crowd you drew before, and they're looking forward to having you back," he said. "The timing is perfect. We'll have full-page ads covering you at both the Jaragua and the bullfight. Now, are you ready for *this*? Walter Winchell and Dorothy Kilgallen are picking it up for their syndicated columns, and *Life* magazine is going to cover it."

"Hot damn, Stanley! I'm ready."

✳ ✳ ✳

Diana and I took off in high spirits. This was the first time I had gone to Mexico by car, but thanks to the Eisenhower administration's 40,000-mile interstate system, we enjoyed every minute of the drive. And since the advent of the new highways, fine motels and restaurants popped up everywhere along the way.

The passion and desire Diana and I had for each other when we'd first met had remained the same, as though our time apart had never occurred. In fact, our love was even deeper now. She was what so many women would like to be: beautiful, extremely sensual, yet childlike at times. As the car wound over the roads, I'd catch a glimpse of her body moving with rhythmic grace to a Spanish ballad on the radio. She'd return my glance with a flirty smile that would warm any heart. And my heart was ready. It had been ages since I had known such happiness.

Traveling from New York to the Texas border took three days. We found Mexico to be a romantic country, a land of strong contrasts, of scorching light and bitter darkness.

Watching Diana's display of carefree joy, I felt the need to look out for her safety—the same feeling of responsibility I'd felt years ago for my grandmother. I laughed, thinking of the self-appointed position I'd taken at age 4. Now, at 31, I felt that same protectiveness for Diana. I didn't want a harsh wind to blow on her or muss her hair. She would be safe now.

As we approached Mexico City, my excitement grew: One of my hidden fantasies was about to come to life. With hard work and determination I could do it.

The 4,000-acre Arruza ranch was a few hours from Mexico City, minutes out of Toluca. As I drove through the Mexican countryside, sobering thoughts awakened in me. I had just two months to learn enough basic passes to oppose the charge of a bull. I knew Stanley's plan sounded great in theory and that it would help my career, but while he was in New York promoting me, I'd be risking my life. Still, Arruza was a good teacher, and I had to have faith in that.

Unaware of my worries, Diana had fallen fast asleep beside me. Now she was being jostled awake by the unpaved road as I drove up to Arruza's ranch. We saw a white stucco house with a red Spanish-tiled roof, a picture of a typical Mexican ranch. A fountain stood in front, encircled by a patio, where ranch hands on horseback greeted us.

We spotted Arruza standing in the doorway, his skin tanned from years of outdoor action. He sported a youthful smile surrounded by slight age lines. Now in his mid 30s, he looked 25 in washed-out jeans and a checked shirt. When we approached the house, Arruza extended his hand and said, "Welcome to Pastaje." His wife, Marl, also came to greet us and invited us inside.

There are two things about Pastaje that I remember well.

One was the enormous dining room, with a table that looked 25 feet long. The other, hanging in the great room, was an enormous painting of Arruza in the ring with a monster of a bull that appeared to be coming headlong out of the canvas. That sight alone was enough to freeze me in my tracks.

Dear God, I thought. *What the hell am I doing?* I felt icy chills up my back, and it took every ounce of my strength to keep from turning around and forgetting the whole damn thing, but it was too late for that.

We were shown to the guest room, where servants had placed our luggage and lit fires in the fireplaces.

* * *

The next morning the training began. In perfect English with only the slightest Spanish accent, Arruza explained, "Bullfighting is a science that takes years to perfect. In executing the passes, one must anticipate the bull and develop the artistry. The flawless grace of a matador in the ring can be earned only through thousands of hours of toil."

Holding two capes, he handed one to me, keeping the other for himself. After demonstrating a Veronica pass, he looked at me and motioned for me to try. I moved to mimic his pass and returned his glance. It wasn't what he wanted. He was quick to explain the difference.

Over the next few days Arruza described the passes he wanted me to learn, then painstakingly broke each one down into fine detail. As I attempted to imitate him, he evaluated my efforts by prompting, coaching, and chastising my clumsy beginnings. He ended each session with the consolation that "a mistake is a good teacher."

Next was the practice with the *muleta* until lunchtime. After a light meal, we were back at it again. No *siesta* for me.

Diana made daily trips to the city and stayed busy browsing in the shops. At night she'd massage my sore muscles, until, nearly exhausted, I'd fall into a deep sleep. Each morning, breakfast was followed by a half-hour session of calisthenics, to stretch tendons and limber up muscles.

The ranch hands, carrying a pair of horns mounted on a stick to simulate the bull's head, took turns charging at me while I executed the passes.

Even practicing a simple formal pass was trying, as I had to learn to pivot on my heels, bringing the back foot forward in a continuous series of movements. It didn't take long to tire while working hour after torturous hour with the heavy cape and *muleta* in the hot sun. My right arm and wrist were sore, my forearm was swollen, and my leg cramps at night were unbearable. Every morning I'd awaken with new aches and bruises. My muscles cried out for a day of rest, but I had to be as relentless as my teacher. There was no time, or need, to learn all the passes, but Arruza wanted me to master those I did learn.

Next it was time to work with the mechanized bull, a large wheelbarrow apparatus with a bull's head mounted on the front and a long metal tube placed where the shoulder blades would be. This was used to practice the kill. To me, this was merely another phase of practice.

Ranch hands know how bulls think and react; they move exactly as a bull would react, no more, no less. If they know what they're doing, they can run with the mechanized bull, roll it, turn it, and hook an amateur with it.

The ranch hands played fair. When they nipped me with a horn, it was because I was wrong. They taught me to be afraid of not being good.

During mealtimes and even while resting after dinner, Arruza continued to teach me. "Learning to control the cape is the cornerstone of the matador's art," he told me. "In the Veronica pass, the cape must be held low in both hands, palms up, and timed slowly just ahead of the horns to bring the animal gracefully around the bullfighter's body. To me, this classic pass is the most elegant of all. The outside tip of the cape must be handled perfectly in order to attract the outside eye of the bull. Even a little wind can multiply the problems of control."

As he spoke, I heard a *clip-a-clop, clip-a-clop* from the horses as they walked along the brick areas outside. "One of the most graceful passes with the *muleta* is the *natural*," Arruza continued. "Its simplicity is what makes it so graceful. The red cloth held in the left hand brings the animal close to his adversary. With a brave bull, the matador can pivot on his heel, do an about-face, and repeat the pass. This is truly an elegant look. With stature and poise, the bullfighter's body blends with that of the bull. This is sublime in motion. Around they go, creating a circle of danger."

One morning, after breakfast, we piled into "El Jeep" and drove to Arruza's private bullring. Today I was to work with the real thing. Not a little calf, like the ones I'd tested in the *tientas*, but a heifer who had already proven her colors and courage.

The ring was enclosed by a stucco wall and a *barrera* at least six feet high, and surrounded by tall pines. There were risers for spectators, away from danger, speckled with ranch hands, visitors, and little boys. Every boy in Mexico seemed interested in bullfighting.

Diana, openly nervous, hugged me tightly. "Be careful, honey," she said. "Please."

"Don't worry. I will."

Scanning the seating area, I pointed to a place at the opposite side of the ring, high above harm's way. With a reassuring nod, Diana made a dash in that direction, her camera in hand. Arruza called out to a ranch hand in Spanish, and they left to bring in the animal.

While we waited, he warned me, "If you move the cape too slowly, the animal will step on it, yank it out of your hands, and gore you. If you move it too fast, you'll remove the lure from his vision and he'll see only you—which could be disastrous."

So many rules, so many warnings, but I listened and learned—my life depended upon it.

"Whatever happens," Arruza continued, "be firm. Don't vacillate. Don't give an inch or the animal will sense your indecision and be on you instantly." He walked with me behind the *burladero,* a wooden shield directly in front of an opening in the *barrera.* There was just enough space between the *burladero* and the *barrera* for a person to squeeze in sideways, but not enough for the bull's horns.

Arruza gave an order to the ranch hands, and they released a 500-pound heifer. She was wild with her new freedom, charging in a zigzag, her head twisting in every direction. The men watched, waiting for an approval or rejection of the animal from Arruza. He shook his head in disapproval; the heifer's movements were too scattered.

As soon as the animal was coaxed out of the ring, another came bounding through the *toril* door. As I waited with Arruza, he was silent for the first time, and I felt the seriousness of the moment.

This one was larger, weighing at least 700 pounds. She kept running in short charges, head down, hooves pawing the ground. This was no ordinary animal: She was looking for a fight.

Arruza studied her, appeared satisfied, and nodded to me.

"For me?" I asked.

"*Si.*"

This was the most penetrating "yes" ever spoken to me. I tried to recall each detail of Arruza's instructions. Of all the experiences I'd had in my life, this moment was the most frightening. Onstage I could always handle an audience. I knew if I ever hit a wrong note, I'd be booed offstage. Here, one wrong move and I could be killed.

Watching the heifer, I slid out from behind the *burladero* and walked toward her as I had been instructed. Sighting her, I called "Uh-hah!" while my throat went dry and my insides tightened. With her head lowered, she pawed the ground. My blood ran hot and pounded against my eardrums. She came fast, hooves blurring as her pace quickened. My brain couldn't distinguish between the pounding of my heart and the thunder of her hooves. She was on me now! The feel of the breeze going by was almost enough to make me faint on the first pass. *Two steps forward,* I told myself, recalling Arruza's instructions.

"Hold out the cape! That's right, move it out!" Arruza yelled. And I felt the heifer's body as she rushed by.

I did it! I did it! I said to myself as relief washed over me. But my joy was short-lived: She turned and came hurtling toward me, and I thought, *Dear God, here she comes again.* Once more I took two steps forward and this time wrapped the cape around my back in a *remate;* again she missed me. I was still standing. I wanted to run, but I forced myself to the security of the *barrera.* Arruza grabbed my shoulder and with a big smile said, "You will never have to be that brave again in your whole life."

My fear evaporated upon my seeing Arruza so pleased. I was proud to have passed my first test and couldn't wait to get into the ring to learn more. Seeing Arruza's smile encouraged me to ask, "Can I try again?" as I wiped the sweat from my face.

"*Sí,* but this time, try the *Gaonera.* Use the cape from behind you. Also, take her farther away from the wall. You're working her too close to the *barrera,* and that's dangerous. But this is natural for a beginner. That wooden fence is like a safety valve; an emergency exit makes it easier to confront danger when one has more guts than experience. Usually a bull will tend to turn away from the fence while he's charging. However," he warned, "there are those that do not, and if you're too close to the fence and your bull likes to swerve into it, you could be impaled upon it."

His words indelible in my mind, I reentered the practice ring excited as hell,and much more confident, even arrogant. I was learning moment by moment, and now I could stand tall. My steps and voice were firm this time as I called to the heifer, "Uh-hah!" She wheeled around and looked in my direction. In a moment she was thundering even faster at me.

I commanded myself to stay still. She lowered her head,

and as she approached, I could smell her sweat. She came much closer; we brushed each other as I pulled my stomach in tightly. She made a tight turn and came at me again. She had to see the lure. The cape! My only chance of making it. I worked the cape, which caught her attention.

While I executed passes in the sand of the arena, she was working well. She was brave, and I was happy with her. *Can't get too happy,* I thought. *Don't underestimate her. Even a heifer is dangerous.* Head down, she pawed the earth again and came at me in her fiercest charge yet.

Working to control the outside corner of the cape, I confronted the animal. Again she charged, and again I stepped forward to meet the charge, learning to turn her at my command. *"¡Olé, señorita!"* cried the ranch hands. I had made it! My first *olé*!

I relaxed when I was safely out of the ring, proud and happy it was over at last. Only then was I aware of my fatigue. Arruza pointed to the Jeep. "No more, Jan. It's been a good day's work in any language."

Diana came running to the car and jumped in, and I eased in beside her. Throwing my head back on the seat, I felt sweat run down my face and neck. As Arruza drove toward the ranch, the cool breeze on my face was refreshing. When we got to the house, I used my last bit of effort to slip into a warm tub, and slowly I began to relax.

I wanted to be able to perfect these passes. As a woman, I felt I had to be a little bit better to win the same acceptance. It was a man's world and a man's game, but I wanted to learn to do it correctly. I had to. All the hours of hard work would be a small price to pay for an achievement so grand.

Diana finally seemed a little more relaxed. "Jan," she said in her excitement, "you looked fantastic. It was so smooth—you hardly moved."

"Thank you. But, my dear," I said, laughing, "I was simply frozen to the damn spot!"

Diana expressed her fears and concerns over my fight in

the Dominican Republic. She had become an astute observer of the practice ring. She missed no detail and was forever busy making a photographic record of my training. "Jan," she said, "I feel so helpless. All I can do is pray."

During Arruza's evening discussions at the main house, Diana followed the accounts of famous bullfights to the last detail. It was obvious this was no frivolous interest for her.

As I settled into the routine of training, Diana found us a pleasant house to rent by the month. It came complete with a housekeeper, whose husband would do the heavy work. There was a fireplace in every room and a houseboy to keep the fires blazing late into the evening.

The hot days were challenging, but the crisp nights were made for slumber. Hard physical work was trimming and toning my body. On Arruza's orders, I ate steak and tomatoes for breakfast, followed by hard work, steak and tomatoes for lunch, then more hard work, steak and work and steak and more work. I was getting stronger, healthier, and showing improvement, and Arruza was pleased with my progress.

Every other week Stanley phoned to report how the plans were progressing for the bullfight at the International Fair and to see if I was still alive. New York seemed like another world, as I was fast becoming a part of the hot circle of sand at Pastaje.

Arruza continued his daily lessons. "A bull is smart," he advised. "A fighter can work with him no longer than 20 minutes. By then the bull has learned exactly where to plunge his horns to find the matador behind the cape. The bull's single desire is to impale the man with his horns and stop the action. Every bullfighter fears a cowardly bull, since it is unpredictable. It can shy off or hesitate at any moment. It may stop inches away, only to attack a heartbeat later, making simple passes dangerous or impossible."

He went on to explain that since brave bulls are bred to fight, their genes urge them to attack anything that moves. They charge straight and true—a symphony in motion, devastatingly beautiful in their grace of execution.

He spoke as though his own mentor had branded the words into his mind. "Still, however brave or cowardly, once an animal has been used in a fight, he becomes too wise and must die," Arruza explained. "In the bullring, the end comes quickly and in glory. Good bull or bad, the poor will eat well, for here the beef is distributed to the hungry."

The weeks were passing quickly, and many details remained to be completed if I were to be ready for the bullfight. I already had the three most important pieces of gear: my sword, *muleta,* and working cape, called the *capa de brega.* This was a full, heavy cape made of raw silk that was dyed bright pink. The lining was thick yellow canvas, and the finished cape was so stiff it would stand by itself. The weight of the cape made me appreciate the strength of the matador's hands and wrists.

For weeks I continued my strict training schedule. I couldn't afford to stop. My best defense was knowledge; not having it could cost me my life.

One evening after practice, Arruza broke the big news. "So far, you've been training with heifers," he said. "But before the fight in the Dominican Republic, you'll have to fight a full-grown bull. My main concern is honing your skill in an actual ring before the fight at the Fair. I must feel confident that you are ready. If you're not ready, it is up to me to correct your mistakes."

This came as a complete surprise to me. I could understand that he felt responsible for my ability, but I hadn't planned on fighting a bull in Mexico. And, Arruza reminded me, Mexican bullfights are not bloodless, as they are in the Dominican Republic; I would have to kill the animal. My only salvation was that I had stayed too busy to anticipate what I was walking into.

Weeks later, Arruza set the date for the first fight in the little town of San Miguel de Allende. Since this fight was to be in Mexico, it would be less expensive to rent a simple bullfighter's suit to wear in the ring: the standard short gray jacket—similar to a bolero—and black trousers, finished off with a frilled Mexican wedding shirt and a vest.

The fight at the International Fair would be much bigger and grander. I wanted to wear the sequin-embroidered suit that all bullfighters wear—the suit of lights, called the *traje de luces*—but I learned that women were forbidden to wear it.

That evening alone with Diana, I was practicing in the center of the living room. The more I thought about not being allowed to wear the suit, the more I expressed my fury. "Why? Why is the suit different for women?" I asked.

"It's just another way to keep us in our places," Diana said.

"But I'll be risking my life the same as them. If I'm gored, my blood is just as red. Isn't a woman in the ring just as brave?" The more I thought about it, the angrier I became and the harder I practiced. Diana could only sit and watch.

"Who in God's name made these damn rules that women have to live by?" I fumed. "And what in the hell do we have to do to be equal? Can't we even offer our lives equally? No, I suppose not."

Diana kept me cool and tried to make sense out of the unfairness of it all. Making the best of the situation, I decided to rent a gray country suit for my first fight. For the Fair, I would need a formal *traje corto*, the suit with a short jacket, which would have to be custom-tailored. For this outfit, Arruza directed me to a haberdasher on the Plaza de la Constitución in Mexico City, where a tailor carefully noted I wanted a white suit. It would have been presumptuous to wear a white suit for my first fight in Mexico, but the International Fair was another matter.

Even if I couldn't wear one in the bullring, I decided I wanted a suit of lights to be used for publicity. On inquiring where to find a tailor, I was directed to a small village, over rough, dry clay roads, and was given the address of a Mexican-Indian woman who specialized in sewing the details on this type of garment. I drove slowly over dirt roads, hampered by blinding dust and the constant rocking of the car. The adobe buildings, which were few, marked the center of the village. The woman I was looking for, however, was said to live in a hut with a thatched roof. I knew communicating with her would be difficult, but I never dreamed it would be nearly impossible.

It was such a day of fun for Diana and me as we stumbled around with the few Spanish words we knew. Trying to find the address of the woman, we approached a boy who pointed to a hut up, over, and around the road across the way. We drove on, stopping at a lumpy stick-and-clay building with a thatched roof.

Through a doorway of sorts, I saw stark-white bedsheets spread over a clay floor. Four girls, about 12 or 13 years old, were sitting on the sheets sewing beaded handwork on suits for bullfighters. Each suit was a different color. Remarkably, even under such crude conditions the material and suits were immaculate.

I tried for some time to relay to the woman my desire to own a suit of lights. *"No comprendo,"* she said. Again I tried to explain. She smiled, saying, *"Si,"* confirming that she would make the suit for me, but quickly added, *"No comprendo."* I was positive she had never made a *traje de luces* for a woman.

At last, despite my broken Spanish, we settled important matters such as fabric and color selection. The *traje de luces* would be made of white silk, heavily encrusted with gold beads, sequins, and braidwork. The inner lining of the jacket would be filled with stiffening material and molded to a precise shape over a body form. When worn in the ring, the suit would offer nothing in the way of protection, despite its stiffness. The jacket alone would be hot and heavy, and the total weight of the complete outfit would be close to 20 pounds. After showing me a calendar, the woman made me understand that the full suit would take six weeks to make, require three fittings, and cost $1,200. She beamed with pleasure as we reached our agreement and was positively glowing when I paid the deposit. Several girls helping with the sewing tried to hide their snickers at the strange American women.

✳ ✳ ✳

As the weeks passed and the date of my first real fight drew nearer, my fears mounted. I tried to work off my anxiety in the practice ring by pushing myself unmercifully. Diana remained quiet.

The night before the fight, I practiced passes with an imaginary bull in our bedroom after Diana had fallen asleep. I worked the animal up and down and around the room until at last, exhausted, I quietly slipped into bed and fell asleep almost the moment my head touched the pillow. It was a deep and dreamless slumber.

Upon awakening, I looked into the darkness of the room and then remembered that today was the day. Startled, I sat upright in bed. My first need was for concentration and prayer. Arruza's warnings and rules kept flashing in my brain. Then came a small reassuring thought: *If I'm not ready now, I'll never be.* But as I leaned back against the pillow, my mind refused to rest. In a few hours I would be there, and I would have two separate fights today. *Dear God, let the bulls be brave,* I prayed.

Diana was still asleep, in a deep, peaceful slumber. She looked like a goddess when she slept, and I felt fortunate to have her with me. She gave me courage, and I needed her now more than ever. Remaining barefoot so as not to disturb her, I quietly dressed in jeans and a shirt, believing I was ready for this. Slipping out onto the small terrace, I breathed as deeply as possible, even though I was shaking. *You have to be confident,* I told myself, recalling Arruza's words: "An animal will sense your indecision." I couldn't let down all those who were depending on me, but I was frightened as hell.

Hearing rustling from the room, I looked through the doorway and saw Diana's angelic face. She was smiling, indicating a good night's rest. She came toward me, and I felt safe for the moment, trying not to let on how scared I was.

Diana and I had a light breakfast of toast and coffee, even though I would have appreciated a shot of tequila a lot more. I'd been warned not to consume a large meal before a fight, since, should I require it, surgery would be less dangerous on an empty stomach.

It was early dawn when I returned to the bedroom and closed the door in order to spend some time alone. Through the window I saw small fires where the poor stayed warm at night and cooked breakfast at daybreak. Nearby, one family, still wrapped in their *rebozos,* huddled by a campfire.

Arruza had warned me that Mexico's high altitude would make breathing while under stress difficult, so he had suggested daily exercises to condition my lungs. Since my arrival at Pastaje, I had been heeding his words. This day, standing on the terrace, I heard marimba music coming from the distant hills while I practiced deep-breathing exercises as I had for my first vocal lesson, taking 10 to 20 deep breaths and holding them. What a difference 20 years makes. At 10, I had learned breath control to sing. At 31, I was sucking in air as if it were my last.

"This is just a little country fight today," I told myself out loud. "Something like an audition. There will be no paid attendance, no big aficionados to dedicate the bulls to." Perhaps if I talked while dressing, I could keep my nervousness under control. I dressed carefully and checked every detail, making sure there wasn't a wrinkle in my shirt or a speck on my suit. I took one last look in the mirror and said, "OK, by damn, you'd better show me what you're made of now." Then I heard a tap on the door.

"Are you ready?" Diana asked.

"Yes."

"Honey, the car is waiting."

"I'll be there." Hesitating, I prayed silently: *Please, God, walk with me.*

When fear whispers, confidence must shout, so I stiffened my back and unlatched the door.

As we neared the bullring in San Miguel de Allende, celebrants, music, and laughter filled the streets. As the car bumped slowly over the cobblestones, I recalled a time when the cobblestone streets themselves were my biggest challenge.

In a glance, I saw Diana. She was vibrant, alive, happy, and wore an air of undisguised love. Thank God she was there.

As I stepped from the car, a shout went up—"*¡Torera!*"— and was repeated again and again. There had been only two other American women bullfighters in the world before me, and the crowd was eagerly awaiting today's fight. Just knowing they were pulling for me helped alleviate my fear.

I was curious to know what kind of bulls were fighting today, but I couldn't ask to see them, since that was considered bad luck. The bulls were chosen well in advance, their names drawn from a hat by the leader of my *cuadrilla*, the team who would assist me. A member of the *cuadrilla* would work the bulls first, and then I could see how the animals charged.

San Miguel de Allende had a small bullring, but we had a procession nonetheless, with the crowd cheering us along. It was so splendid, I wanted to stop the minutes from passing. Instead, time seemed to jump, and suddenly I was standing behind the *barrera*, watching the *toril* door. The hot sun beating on the sand reflected onto my face, but the sweat on my brow came more from nerves than the heat. Now I really needed that tequila.

A trumpet blared. The bullpen door opened, and out charged Ambulancia. What a name for my first bull. Head high, he looked first right, then left. The bull was alert, his turns quick. He made short charges at nothing, just for the hell of it. One of my *cuadrilla* ran out and moved the animal around with his cape. This was a brave fighting bull with a thousand years of combat bred into his soul; he charged at anything that offered a fight. There could only be one bull this magnificent and brave on the list, and he was mine.

I waved my *cuadrilla* aside and walked alone into the ring, feeling equal to the men around me. Catching Ambulancia's attention, I spoke quietly. "OK, come on. Uh-hah! Come on! Uh-hah!" In a blink of the eye he was after me, hooves pounding the sand like a locomotive, louder and louder as he bounded across the ring. An audible gasp rose from the crowd as the bull breezed past me.

As the animal turned, the mound of muscles in his neck glistened in the late-afternoon sun. *Keep his attention fixed on the outside tip of the cape,* Arruza had told me. *Work the tip of the cape to take the bull out! Move forward, Jan, here he comes! Hard, fast, closer and closer. The bull's turning. Here he is! Control him! Control him!* I went with my *remate,* swirling the cape with such force that it stood out like the skirt of a dancer.

"*¡Olé!*" shouted the crowd. "*¡Olé, torera! ¡Torera Americana!*"

My courage soared, and back I went. This time holding the cape behind me, I relaxed one hand against the small of my back, the other end of the cape extended to the side and just slightly toward the animal in the classic *Gaonera.* It was dangerous; I was in full view of the bull. The outside corner of the cape caught Ambulancia's eye, and when I moved forward, calling him, the bull lowered his head and charged toward me. I turned on my heels without moving my feet or body so as to lead his horns into the folds of the cape; the bull stopped his charge inches from the lure. I moved the outside corner of the cape, but the animal failed to charge. He just took one step forward and stopped. I was in trouble: The bull was just inches away. Ambulancia's fiery eyes followed the outside edge of the cloth upward to my right hand, across my arm, and looked into my eyes. This bull was wise, and I was vulnerable. My muscles tightened; I refused to flinch.

Looking steadily at me, the animal moved forward. Then, twisting his head and pointing his horns toward me, he butted into my body. Panic shot through my body. With a terrorizing blow, Ambulancia hooked his horn between my thighs, flinging me off my feet. Then, with a sudden jerk, the bull pulled his head upward in a swift whipping action, turned me into the air, and slammed my body onto the ground with a devastating blow. The force rushed the air from my lungs, and I lay on the hot sand feeling like the cartilage had dislodged from my bones.

As I lay there, I listened to the snorting above me and was momentarily shocked into rigidness. The boys of the *cuadrilla* ran quickly toward me. *"¡Calla te!"* they screamed. "Be quiet! Be quiet!" Fear and cold reality came over me.

Don't move, I told myself, fighting for the courage to remain immobile. As I lay facedown, my teeth were gritty with sand, and I could taste and feel the gorge rising in my throat. I felt warm air jetting from Ambulancia's nostrils onto the back of my neck; the animal was that close to me. Holding my breath, I waited for the great horns to rip me open. The loose skin on his huge mouth flapped as he snorted, and the strings of his saliva ran down my neck. The stench was enough to make me vomit.

From a distance I heard the *cuadrilla* calling, *"¡Toro! ¡Toro! ¡Ah, ah, toro!"* Finally, I felt the beast's hooves brush over my back and heard them drumming away. His thunder shook the earth. I jumped to my feet, angry and hurt. Only one of us could win. *By damn, it's going to be me,* I thought.

Once again I had the bull's attention. My eyes pierced the animal like torches of death. "You bastard," I murmured. "I'm ready for you now. Uh-hah! Come on!" The bull came toward me, and we fought together. I had to outwit him. I was mad, but I had to control it. Anger in the ring is dangerous.

There on the sand we struggled for life. The brute was bent on destroying me, on stopping my movement, like a cat on a moth. Around and around the ring we fought, the blood-red *muleta* flashing in the sunlight. I had to dominate. I was doing simple passes, *naturals,* and he was passing painfully close—so close I felt the barrel of his rib cage as he turned into me. The crowed had come to see a fight, and by damn, that's what they were getting.

In command now, I remained nearly immobile in order to lead the bull with the lure of the *muleta*. I finished with a *pase de pecho,* then walked to the safety of the *barrera* with calm tenseness. Our moment of truth had arrived. The bull was waiting, looking at me. I had to go after him fairly, straight in over the horn as I had practiced. But in practice it had all seemed so automatic—all those hundreds of hours with the sword and tube. As I'd practiced getting the proper aim, running the sword into the bull, I never actually allowed myself to realize what it would be like to kill when the time came. I'd been concerned primarily with learning the necessary skills and remembering details. Following the rules, I'd aim for the spot between the shoulder blades and plunge the sword into the practice tube. Time after time I worked to perfect my skill, and time after time I'd hit my target.

But now I had to push the sword through the bull's flesh and into his heart and watch as blood flowed onto the sand. If I refused, the bull would still die, but at the hands of the *cuadrilla.* So I moved from behind the barrera to the center of the ring with the *muleta* and sword and walked straight toward the magnificent animal. We were face to face in the ring.

In my head I heard Arruza's repeated warning: *The animal's feet must be together in order to separate the shoulder blades. If his feet are apart, the shoulder blades will come together and the sword will hit bone. This can throw the sword six feet into the air, leaving you defenseless.*

There in the ring, as I moved the outside tip of the red cloth, the bull's eyes followed my movement. Then he lowered his head and brutally charged toward me. Eyeing the length of the sword, I set my sights on the kill spot as the animal came closer and closer. Then my blade found its target.

As I reached over the bull's head, his horns flipped the edge of my jacket. Self-preservation motivated the initial plunge, but with each fraction of a second the action became more and more difficult as my heart and mind became involved, asking, *What am I doing?* Then in an instant came a saving thought: *Do it! Do it right or he'll suffer.* So I plunged the sword into the bull's body, deeper and deeper until, with his last breath, he let out an agonizing scream.

Thank God it was over quickly. Engrossed in my own thoughts, I was unaware of the crowd or their cheers. All other senses stopped as I walked away and Ambulancia was hauled out of the arena.

The second bullfighter of the day was in the ring before I realized it, and he was doing well. Exhausted, I wanted to go home. Was I strong enough to go into the ring again and face another bull? Then came a vivid picture of Grandma as she sent me out to face a much smaller enemy. She had washed the blood from my knees and made me straighten my back and stand up to the fight. But it's difficult to stand up to the fight when there is no enemy.

I watched the second bullfighter closely. He was down on his knees, then up again, executing graceful passes with his cape. He placed his *banderillas* well. Damn. He was good, and the half-smile on his face when he looked at me told me he knew it.

What could I do with my second bull to equal him? I had used my entire repertoire in my first match. With each passing moment, I felt more nauseous. The sun was growing hotter, and I was ready to throw up when I heard his bull cry and fall dead.

The trumpet blared too soon. As I looked at the *toril* door, out blasted my second bull like a shot. Everything but what was inside the circle disappeared. As a bullfighter, there's no room for any other thoughts in your world. The bull is your only world until it's over and you step back into reality.

I can't recall all the details of the second fight, but at one point, in trying to hold my own with the other matador, I went down on my knees. The animal passed so close to me that the side of his horn grazed my neck, and I felt the sting of my own sweat in the open cut. From there I worked the rest of the fight as proudly as I had been taught, but from a standing position. I remember the bull charging and brushing by with his full length while I sucked in my stomach. The animal saw the lure, and I watched as he wheeled around me to do it again, creating a circle of fear.

For the moment of truth, I threw every ounce of my 126 pounds onto the blade. The sword found its mark, and instantly the bull stepped out, separating his front feet and closing his shoulder blades onto the sword. I felt the blade cut deeper and deeper as I numbed myself to the animal's excruciating pain. An awful stench rose in the air as the bull's blood oozed slowly at first then came in spurts. The smell baked into my nostrils as I cut harder, through muscle and sinew, into the bellowing bull.

As I pushed the sword, my mind screamed with questions: *What have I turned into? Dear God, has ambition made me this hard?* As tears filled my eyes, I prayed that the bull would die quickly. My love for animals was far too strong for this. I knew the bull would have killed me had I made the wrong move, but somehow that reasoning wasn't enough.

The giant bull was down on his knees and alive, in tremendous pain: I had botched the kill. Looking into his eyes, I remembered the pleading eyes of all the dogs I had saved from animal shelters. *What's so different now?* I wondered. *This animal is hurting. Please, God, let him die quickly.*

As I looked at the bull through more pain and fear than I had ever felt for anything, one of my *cuadrilla* came running to me with a dagger to end it all quickly. After it was over, I stood motionless, looking down at the bull, grieving deeply for the life I had taken.

In practice, I had only been concerned with saving my life. Thinking only of the art, I never once asked myself if I could kill the animal. Now I knew I had the heart to compete, the heart to succeed, but the heart to kill? No. I could never do it again. Suddenly the fight in the Dominican Republic and everything it could do for my career seemed trivial.

I stood up straight and walked from the ring as the crowd's cheers rang in my ears. Marimba music started immediately as I walked, holding my hat high in the air, my feelings mixed. I felt tormented because of the killing, yet proud for having accomplished the art of the fight and having conquered my fear. The celebration looked like Mardi Gras, with people in masks and painted faces calling to me. I spotted Diana rushing through the hordes of spectators, smiling and jubilant that I was alive. I held her tightly, unconcerned with the crowd around us. As I released her, hundreds of people gathered around, asking me to sign their programs. The celebration continued with balloons, fireworks, and costumed dancers.

The bull breeder of San Miguel de Allende approached and invited Diana and me, along with the entire *cuadrilla*, to have dinner with him. Two members of my *cuadrilla* escorted us through the masses to the dining room, which was within walking distance.

The room was immense. Covering the walls were pictures of famous matadors, and in the center of the room stood a 20-foot-long banquet table. I was seated at the head of the table, with the breeder at the other end—too far away to converse, even if we had both spoken the same language. *"¡Torera!"* the guests shouted. Glasses and bottles of *cerveza* and tequila clinked with a toast to my "health, money, and love." The horrors of the day over, I was accepted and praised for what I had accomplished.

On the wall, 10 feet behind me, hung one of my bulls. I glanced at the animal and quickly looked away, feeling nauseous. Even though this trophy was intended as a gracious gesture, I thanked God that the day was behind me.

Darkness settled on San Miguel de Allende while the smoke of the cooking fires carried a rich fragrance throughout the room and strains of mariachis played faintly in the distance. This night I felt grateful beyond measure, and wiser and older by a hundred years.

With the mission in Mexico accomplished, Diana started packing the car for our trip back to the States, and I placed a call to Stanley in New York.

"Jan," he said, "We've been busy making contacts with Felix Soya, the P.R. man in Ciudad Trujillo."

"Terrific, Stanley. What's going on? Anything new?"

"Well, Soya stressed the importance of drawing American tourists down there to ensure the success of the Fair."

"What's the problem? There are always tons of Americans down there."

"Evidently not lately," Stanley said. "Soya said the tourist trade has been rapidly decreasing. Trujillo's advisers in the States center much of the blame on negative publicity surrounding the Trujillo regime that's being circulated in print throughout the States. More and more Americans have been frightened into staying home."

"The bullfight should do it, Stan."

"That's what Soya thinks too," he said. "But he's getting anxious."

"I just thank God the fight will be bloodless."

"Yeah, let's just hope the bull knows the rules."

"Thanks," I said laughing. "I really needed that."

In the background, Stan's office sounded like a rat race, so we quickly ended the conversation. Diana and I finished packing the station wagon, looking forward to our journey home.

As we crossed the border in Brownsville, Tex., on March 19, 1956, the sun shone brightly, and the fast-moving highway aimed us toward New York City. Once we had arrived at the apartment, I had roughly a week to prepare for the fight in the Dominican Republic. Diana left New York to spend some time with her parents and Jami, and to make further arrangements for our trip. I had a long list of things to do: send my gowns out to be cleaned, pay the apartment rent in advance, reserve a garage space—the list went on and on.

Everything had been arranged through General Trujillo's right-hand man, General De Moya. The bullfight at the International Fair was set and on schedule. I spent every free moment practicing with my cape and *muleta*.

Arruza's words were imbedded in my brain: *You must keep strong and limber. It would be foolish to allow your muscles to soften and have to go through the pain of limbering again.* In addition, I had to continue vocalizing to keep my voice in condition, since I was also scheduled to sing in the Dominican Republic. With time running out, however, I was compelled to practice both at the same time.

While singing and working with the cape to keep limber, I was torn between the way I looked and sounded and the way I felt inside. I wanted desperately to let the audience know who I was. I wanted to say to them, *Look at me. This is who I am and this is how I sound. Now, please like me as a person.* Then an idea struck me. By wearing the bullfight suit underneath a long gown, I could perform my regular act, then go offstage and return dressed in the suit of lights. Without frills, earrings, or yards of netting, the audience could see the real me. I'd finish with a strong number, and they'd surely know.

Without expressing my reason, I told Morry my idea.

"Sounds terrific," he said. "You choreograph the bullfight segment and work on the timing for a quick costume change and work it into your act."

"And after I return from the Dominican Republic, I'll put it in my show and polish it to perfection."

Since the suit of lights was made up of many pieces—shirt, vest, cummerbund, tie, pants, and shoes—a quick change would be difficult and would require several performances to smooth out the rough spots. I could wear the pants underneath my gown, but anything more would be too bulky.

Diana helped with the choreography when she returned to New York. At times during a breather from practice, I'd watch her. I loved watching her move. She had such grace in the simplest everyday movements: reaching for a cup of coffee, putting on an earring or a pair of hose. I was deeply in love with her, and her love for me helped see me through the pressure.

On April 1, 1956, Diana and I boarded a plane at Idlewild Airport and flew to Miami, where the Navy took us to Guantánamo Bay, Cuba, for one week to entertain the servicemen and women at the Naval Air Base there.

The following week, Diana and I left for Ciudad Trujillo. A quick glance at the other passengers on the plane told us we were the only Americans onboard. We saw the Island of Hispaniola, east of Cuba and Jamaica, from the air. The Dominican Republic is located at the eastern part of the island, while Haiti is on the western side.

What a welcome we received. We were met at the airport by General De Moya and two guards with fixed bayonets. Arriving at the Hotel Jaragua, I was flattered to be greeted with such grand gesture. An armed soldier stood on either side of the main entrance to the hotel, and there were additional guards in the lobby. Diana raised an eyebrow as we entered, then quipped with a sexy Harlow humor, "Do you suppose they're expecting more excitement than us?"

As General De Moya prepared to leave the hotel, he delivered a message to me from the president, Generalissimo Rafael Leonidas Trujillo, requesting a command performance at 8 o'clock that evening at a function held for guests of the president.

Three hours later guards armed with guns and bayonets escorted us to the limousine that was to take us to San Cristobal, where the function was being held. It was a long, desolate drive into the country.

Upon our arrival, an elevator took us to a small but elaborate ballroom where marble pillars were topped with large gold Ionic designs. On each of the many tables, crystal stemware and carved gold ashtrays complemented the diamonds and jewels of the guests. The ballroom was lavishly decorated in gold and marble, to the point of being gaudy. Clearly, a fortune had been spent on the place. The band was large, and as they began to play, couples in evening clothes made their way to the dance floor. Diana's glance caught mine, and, nodding toward the dancers, she said in somewhat comic derision, "Shall we?"

"We can't," I answered, mocking her tone, "we're not on the guest list." And then I thought, *What a pity, gay people have to dance in the closet.* I would've loved to have danced with Diana, but it wouldn't have been accepted.

Recognizing General Trujillo, I approached him and General De Moya to pay my respects. Trujillo was a large man, stern and intimidating, but courteous. He merely nodded when I addressed him.

During my performance I realized that despite its opulence the ballroom lacked special lighting effects and an adequate public address system. But those details became unimportant in comparison to the welcome response of the audience.

Following my performance, General De Moya suggested firmly, "The guards will escort you to the hotel for your evening show at the Jaragua." We were ushered out as quickly as we were ushered in.

The two guards led us from the car into the lobby and up to our room. I appreciated the protection, although I didn't understand what we were being protected from.

Over the next few days I was interviewed by newspaper reporters from *El Caribe* and *La Nación,* which put out half-page ads announcing "The American Woman Bullfighter." I had never received so much publicity for one show. Every ad, however, brought threatening phone calls to the newspaper and to me, from people who either opposed the bullfighter being a woman, the bullfighter being American, or the bullfight itself.

A few days later, General De Moya informed me that the fight would take place on May 16, which would give me three weeks to practice. Hearing that, I began to relax.

Five hours later, at 3 A.M., an informant delivered a message to the general saying that angry terrorists were planning to kidnap the American woman. De Moya phoned General Trujillo to arrange an immediate meeting.

Diana and I were told we were leaving. Two armed guards flanked the doorway. Speaking to an interpreter, I asked, "Where are we going?" The tension surrounding us was intense.

"The General has offered the use of a house where the two of you can stay and you can practice in private," he explained.

Three main highways led from Ciudad Trujillo; the longest one, which went northward, was 204 miles long. We reached the end of the highway, and then were driven into the country on a narrow road, through large forested tracks of cedar, mahogany, and satinwoods. Soon we were in a remote, dense forest—a jungle to our innocent eyes. Lush vegetation grew in stark contrast to a land utterly barren of human life. There was not a shack or trail, or smoke from a single fire, not even another car on the rough road. The countryside was as unknown as if it had never been explored.

We drove for miles without conversation. Diana nudged me and pointed to the door on either side of us. As she ran her hand over the side door's upholstery, we realized there were no window or door handles in the backseat.

Jokingly she whispered in a sexy tone, "On this dark road in the middle of nowhere, what would keep them from stopping the car and killing us?"

Somehow he dark humor of her question helped ease our tension.

"But without us," I whispered, "what would they do for excitement?"

Every glance from Diana was accented by a raised eyebrow.

The car hummed its way through the country. Looking up the hill to our right where one officer pointed, we saw an elegant two-story country house through the palm trees. Halfway up the driveway, near the path to the servants' quarters, the speeding car roused a flock of chickens, sending them squawking and beating their wings while the driver hit his brakes hard.

A man and woman, the caretakers, came out of the house and nodded as the officer spoke briefly with them. One of the guards informed us that the couple only spoke Spanish. Our bags had barely been unloaded and carried to the house when the car departed. As we listened until the sound of the car had faded away, we knew this would be our last contact with the outside world for some time.

Stepping into the house, I noticed the fine, detailed mosaic tile floors and plush, low white sofas; it seemed the perfect romantic hideaway. Soft lighting filtered through flowing draperies and glass, and floor-to-ceiling windows were every-where. Groups of pillows on white velvet sofas were covered in mink and some in gold brocade. I looked at Diana and knew we shared the same thought: *Boy, what I'd give to have a luxury place like this for us.*

"Beautiful isn't it, Diana?"

"Oh, yes," she smiled. Then, after a quick once-over of the house, she remarked, "I'm certain this is the first time this place has been used to practice bullfighting."

The house sat on a hill surrounded by a stucco wall with locked iron gates at the driveway. It overlooked miles of ter-rain, densely covered with tropical vegetation. As far as the eye could see in any direction, there were no signs of life, no pathway, no people but us. Even the roadway was hidden by the trees. We were completely alone, a slim telephone line our only link to the outside world. Being unable to communicate in Spanish, though, only added to our dilemma.

We went to bed early that night. In our room we listened to the crackling fire and talked about having a home together like the hideaway we were in, after Jami went to college.

Diana sat in bed hugging her knees and propped up against two large satin pillows, while I relaxed on a plush lounge. "You know," she said, pressing her head into the pillow, "there are many weeks during the year that I'm alone. Jami spends a lot of time with Greg's parents, with my mother, and at camp. So you know, I could easily spend time with you throughout the year."

It sounded like a dream come true. "Lately my contracts have been confirmed six months to a year in advance," I said, "so we'd have several months to make plans."

Diana and I talked for some time. But the glow of the fire seemed to soothe her, and after a while I found that I was talking to myself. Relaxing there, I thought about the fight and how thankful I was that it would be bloodless—at least for the bull. The animal was guaranteed to walk away from the ring alive, but me?

I slipped into bed and lay watching the reflection of the fire dance on the ceiling, which sent a red glow flashing about like a devilish matador's cape. Excited and frightened, I prayed to God that I'd get through the fight alive. I couldn't let Diana know I was worried.

$$* \quad * \quad *$$

Early the next morning we were awakened by the crowing of a rooster. The highly polished floor tiles were cold and slick under our bare feet, so we dressed quickly.

After an enjoyable breakfast prepared by the caretakers, I was eager to get started. Therefore, that day I set a tight and demanding schedule for myself. I would start at daybreak, stop for breakfast, then go back to work in the courtyard until the noon meal. After that I'd go back to practicing, working a total of 10 hours a day.

On April 31, General De Moya received a second anonymous threat, this one expressing anger over an American participating in a bullfight in their country. The disgruntled writer vowed to disrupt the fight.

Unaware of this, I practiced daily from morning to night, stopping only to eat, sleep, or rest briefly.

Diana often expressed her boredom. "You know, Jan," she said one day, "other than sitting at the bedroom window watching you practice, I have nothing to do. I smoke and do my nails—that's it. I'd like to write a letter home, but there's no way to mail it. Had I known what to expect, I'd have brought a deck of cards for solitaire. I tried making a phone call to Jami, but the operator couldn't understand me." Laughing, she added, "My greatest challenge each day is hooking my bra."

Every once in a while I'd see Diana pick up the phone and simply listen. When I chuckled at her, she said, "I'd even enjoy a wrong number, just to hear the cheery little bell. Or I'd settle for a book in English—any kind, even an atlas or dictionary."

I tried to think of things to occupy her time, but there weren't any. "That's OK," she'd laugh. "It's almost time to take another bath and redo my makeup."

Several days passed, and still we had no visitors. Diana stood at the window gazing for a long time at the road leading from the house. Finally, she displayed a newly opened pack of cigarettes in her outstretched hand. "See these?" she announced in desperation. "They're all I have left. If I have to give up smoking, you may have to call an ambulance. But I doubt one would come!"

Unknown to us, May 12, four days before the fight, a kidnapping plan had been confirmed, and General Trujillo gave the order to cancel the bullfight. We were quiet, and I was preoccupied with my own silent prayers and fears about the fight when the phone rang.

I heard a woman's soft, pleasant voice speak my name, and listened as she transferred the call to General De Moya.

"*Señorita* Welles?" he said.

"Yes, General."

"*Señorita*, General Trujillo wishes that I inform you that due to circumstances beyond his control, he finds it necessary to cancel the bullfight."

I was so happy, I could hardly answer. I had prayed so hard for this.

"*Señorita* Welles?" he said. "Hello?"

"I'm sorry, General De Moya..."

"I have made travel arrangements for the two of you to

leave the country tomorrow," he told me. "A car will arrive to drive you to the airport at 10 A.M." And in a most gracious way, he apologized for the inconvenience.

We were so relieved that we hurried through our packing like elves preparing for Christmas, and were elated knowing our strange experience was coming to an end. But we had no way of knowing the hell that fate had in store for us.

The next morning the limo in the driveway was a welcome sight. After our seemingly endless drive, General De Moya greeted us at the airport and led us to a plane bound for Miami.

After the plane took off, we relaxed with a drink, and Diana said with a demure, elegant look, "When I write my memoirs I'll tell about the time I was trapped in the jungle while a bull-fighter fought night and day beneath my window!"

We were laughing and so happy to be heading for the States. Looking toward the heavens, I offered my thanks. Although it was the same sky I had seen for the past few weeks, it had never looked bluer.

I was grateful to be out of a situation that could have taken my life if one of many simple things had happened—a cowardly bull, a brave one with poor eyesight, a gust of wind blowing the lure of the cape toward me, a bad day...maybe my last! Now I could go on happily with a renewed hope for the future. At least that was my plan.

* * *

Soon we were back in our home in Forest Hills, New York. People around us didn't appreciate how lucky they were, but we knew. I reported to Morry in Pittsburgh what had occurred and asked him about my bookings.

"Hey, things are happening," he said. "In two weeks you open at Blinstrub's in Boston. After Boston, I got you the Glen Casino in New York, Casino Royal in D.C., Club Elegant in Brooklyn, Barclay Hotel in Toronto, and Elmwood Casino in Windsor, Ontario, for starters. Now, listen to this: I'll have you booked solid for a year, so you can polish the new act. I've also booked you on *The Steve Allen Show* and *To Tell the Truth*. How 'bout that?"

"Terrific, Morry. That's terrific!"

"Wait, I'm not finished! I got the big one for you, Jan! After all the other engagements, you open July 4 for two weeks at the Palace Theater in New York."

It was a dream come true. Words couldn't express my gratitude to Morry for all he had done.

Diana flew back to Louisville for Jami's 12th birthday, to prepare her for boarding school, and to help her pack for summer camp. She had planned to remain there until her daughter was out of school for the summer, then join me on the road at various times over the next three months while Jami was at camp or visiting her grandparents.

Morry had the act booked solid, one engagement following on the heels of the other. Even though the reviews were terrific, some were so full of fluff and femininity that I thought the critics were writing about someone else. *Variety* carried an account of the Barclay Hotel show in Toronto:

> From the whisper style to the big voice treatment, Jan Welles is a trim and talented redhead who has a diversified but disciplined voice. In a black-lace-over-pink strapless evening gown, she is an instant attention getter with her high-voice opening of "High on a Windy Hill." This immediately warmed up the packed room.... From there on in, Miss Welles is a direct click for tempo switches and styling, ranging from the low notes to her alternate stratosphere finals. "No Arms" hushed the room, and her bouncy 'Live Till I Die' in shout style is followed by a low-down "Sing You Sinners.:

As I worked on better timing and lighting, the act grew stronger with each show. *Morry will love it,* I thought, though I was a bit worried since other than receiving contracts in the mail, I never heard from him.

Everything else was going well, and Diana joined me in Windsor, Ontario. Even though I had missed her terribly over the past few weeks, we were living a dream and had never been happier.

In preparation for opening night at the Palace, I dressed in the suit of lights from the waist down, slipped into a floor-length gown from *The Godfrey Show*, and checked the mirror one last time.

Earlier, Diana had gathered her cues for the light man and the curtain man. She gave these notes to the stage manager, then stood beside me until I was ready to walk onstage. While the orchestra played my introduction, I walked to center stage in a blackout. After a moment a spotlight illuminated me. The excitement of the audience grew as I sang each of my numbers for the first part of the act: moving ballads, then mood songs, up-tempos, and finally "power pieces." At the end of the last song the applause began, and the stage went black. Hurriedly, as the ovation continued, offstage I removed my earrings and bracelets and added tight bands to hold back my hair. A dresser unzipped my gown and assisted with the quick change.

The audience was still applauding as the dresser held a mirror in front of me for a final check. While adjusting the jacket, cummerbund, and tie, I heard the master of ceremonies begin the introduction to the bullfight sequence.

"Last Sunday, ladies and gentlemen, in *The New York Mirror* there was a wonderful spread on one of the world's three American girl bullfighters," the announcer said in a grand voice. "The young lady in question has fought in Mexico, with a display of exceptional courage. Now, ladies and gentlemen, if you will sit back, and with the help of your imagination, place yourself in the bullring in Mexico, we would like to introduce you to the young lady as she gives a comprehensive display of the different passes used while fighting a bull. You've seen Jan Welles, the singer. Now prepare to be transported to the Plaza de Toros as we present Jan Welles, *torera*!"

The audience quietly welcomed the sensual, soul-stirring notes of "Malagueña" as I walked into the imaginary bullring with a charging red pinspot simulating the bull. The music bound us together, transporting us to the hot sand of the Mexican bullring late on a Sunday afternoon. Coaxing the imaginary bull's charge, I dropped to my knees. The audience was moved to respond while we shared the tremor of fear and courage as the red pinspot of the phantom bull grazed my side and flashed by the sweeping cape. The light and cape snapped across the stage and I heard "*¡Olé!*" from the balconies. Their cheer rang in my ears as I raised my hat in triumph to acknowledge their applause. The sound of their ovation pulled me from my memories of the dusty ring back to the stage.

Clapping and shouting, everyone rose from their seats. During the applause the orchestra began the introduction to my closing number, "I'm Gonna Live Till I Die." My voice soared to the song's climax, the last note filling the theater, holding the audience tense until they exploded once again with applause. As their shouts of joy washed over me, the lights came up and the sound continued as I took several curtain calls.

Fans delivered gifts backstage after the performance, and Diana was busy answering the phone, which rang constantly. Telegrams were delivered, and flowers arrived and were placed in every available space in the dressing room, at the doorway, and into the hall.

"Jan," Diana said, as the phone rang again, "the callers are so complimentary. They must know what this engagement means to you."

"Well, I feel like I'm standing in the middle of Times Square saying, 'Look at me. I'm a nice person who just happens to be a lesbian!'"

Diana hurried to answer the phone again, and I was filled

with emotion and love for all the good people. There were many of them wearing Jan Welles Fan Club buttons, waiting at the stage door for autographs. And it didn't stop there. Renowned songwriter Nick Kenny came backstage to give me his book of poems, with the inscription "From one redhead to another," and sports writer Lou O'Neill had sent me a copy of Rex Smith's *Biography of the Bulls.*

The next day, Diana and I were in our apartment sorting clothes for the cleaners and laundry, laughing at our adventures over the past 14 months, when we heard a knock at the door. Diana stopped abruptly and straightened her back. The air became still. She followed me into the living room. Her strange reaction caused me to hesitate as I reached for the door.

Standing in the hallway, a 6-foot-tall, attractive, well-dressed gentleman said, "May I see Diana?"

Diana came to the door and stood beside me, and I heard her say, "I told you not to come here. What do you want?"

Turning to me, she said in a disgusted tone, "Jan, this is Greg, my ex-husband."

The moment was awkward. I was stunned but trying not to succumb to discomfort. I said, "Well, invite him in."

With his chin in the air, Greg spoke as if determined to move Diana. "I told you what I wanted when I called last night. I want you back," he said, looking uncomfortable in my presence. I left the room and heard him say, "I visited your mother and Jami, and—"

"Greg, we've settled this in court. I told you I didn't love you when we married. I didn't then, I don't now, and I never will. You and my mother arranged that marriage. Now it's over. Live with it."

"Just a minute," he said in a tone laced with false superiority. "If I were to take you to court and show you for what you are, I could take Jami away from you. Your mother's agreed to back me up if necessary. She'll testify on my behalf regarding your character and the way you've been living. Think about it. I have."

Hearing that, I stormed into the room.

Turning to me, Greg added, "It wouldn't be so good for you either, you know!" He just stood there in his silk summer suit, glaring as I stepped toward him.

"Get out of here, you bastard!" I yelled. "Get out!"

He hesitated, then started for the door. "Diana," he said, speaking firmly through clenched teeth, "you know where to call me, and I suggest you do."

After he left, Diana and I stood there silently, as though a bottomless pit had opened up into which our entire world would drop.

"You knew he was coming?" I asked her.

"He called me last night at the theater and said he was coming. But I didn't believe him because he's always making threats he never carries out. Last night you and I were so happy with the success of the show that I couldn't tell you."

Seeing my pain, Diana tried to comfort me. "Jan, I should never have married that son of a bitch. I know that."

"It's not that you married him. It's that you and I were just beginning to live."

"When I married him I was young," Diana said. "The pressure from my family, friends, neighbors—it was all too much. What I wanted out of life seemed unimportant to everyone but me. Greg was my mother's choice. I told her I never wanted to get married, but she thought marriage would 'cure' the love I had for you. When your mother told her about the letters I sent you, the pressure started. Finally, I married him to shut her up. I was just tired of fighting. For three miserable months I tried to live in his world. After a near breakdown I had to stop trying."

I started to speak, but the words wouldn't come.

"You're different, Jan," Diana said. "You always have been. You've stood up to society. Not many of us are able to do that."

"Diana, you can't hand your life to others and allow them to mold it to their liking. I'm sure you've never asked anyone to live their life according to your rules, so why should you live yours according to theirs? That's asking someone to live a lie. No one has the right to ask that of anyone. Now, tell me, what are you going to do?"

"I'm staying with you," she said, and quickly added, "I don't think Greg will carry out his threat. Perhaps he'll think better of it."

✳ ✳ ✳

At the theater I continued to tap every ounce of my ability to give a performance no one had ever seen before. A few days later, at home, I was trying to relax and put Greg's threats behind us when Diana came in with the mail.

"Greg's taking me to court," she said, "to try to get custody of Jami." In a near whisper, she added, "I have to go."

There was no need to say more. I couldn't have tolerated the pain anyway. I was praying she wouldn't break down, because I had barely enough strength for myself.

From another room I heard her call the airport for the next flight to Louisville, and my small world shattered. As she dressed, applied her makeup, and brushed her hair, I could only watch, and I watched as though I'd never see her again.

That evening, at the airport, we said goodbye. My eyes followed her plane until it was just a speck in the black sky. The night was unforgiving in its quiet.

$\mathcal{e}$ight

I'm Gonna Live Till I Die

I knew the finger-pointing judges of society would never allow Diana to return. She would live like a slave, with a mind trapped, simply because she lived differently than others. The rainbows that once covered my eyes were gone, and I vowed I would keep walking forward. *There's no progress without rebellion,* I thought, *and I will progress.*

With my love for Diana foremost in my mind, I went to the theater. In the lobby I stood between two larger-than-life-size blowups, one of a bullfighter with a cape stopped in motion during a final pass. The other was of a feminine-looking woman, in a gown of silk tulle with sequins and gossamer swirls. *You may not understand my personal life,* I vowed, *but whether you love me or hate me, by damn, you're going to know me.*

That night I hit center stage and gave the audience everything they had come to see and hear, to the point of uninhibited rebellion. Then, rushing from the stage to my dressing room, I pulled off bits of costume to protect them from the sweat rolling down my face and back. I was exhausted. Sitting in the dressing room, wrapped in a terry cloth robe with my feet propped on a chair, I relived the past 18 months, angered at those who had degraded the love Diana and I shared.

It was hot, and the door to the hall was ajar. From the reflection in the dressing-room mirror I spotted a face with a familiar smile peering around the door frame. And then I heard a voice I hadn't heard in 10 years: "Jan, I caught your show. You were dynamite! And ya still got 'em fooled, haven't ya, girl!" Those words didn't register until some time later. At the moment I was too taken aback by the voice and the smile.

"Bobby?"

His smile was still charming and warm, but he looked drawn and in need of a shave, and his clothes were wrinkled. This wasn't the Bobby of my Riviera and Embassy Club days. It was obvious he had been living a different life.

Startled for a moment, I spun in my chair toward his out-stretched arms. My arms opened wide as he came forward and grabbed me tightly.

"Son of a bitch!" I said in disbelief. "Where the hell have you been?" The years hadn't been kind to my former manager, who had once been a lady killer and fashion plate. He pulled up a dressing-room chair and slowly turned toward me, completely ignoring my question.

"I've been following your career all the way," Bobby said.

"I tried for months to contact you."

"Yeah, I had to get out." His expression was dismal. "Things didn't work out the way I wanted. It was getting too rough. I just couldn't get back to you."

As I retouched my makeup for the 5 o'clock show, Bobby continued to talk but offered no further explanation for his years of absence. He had always been an immaculate dresser. From his cologne to his socks, every detail was snappy, sharp, and smart-looking. The change was saddening.

I had so many things to ask, but Bobby dodged questions he didn't want to answer by speaking of casual things, such as my act. Realizing I was ready to change into costume, Bobby stood to leave, then walked toward me and said, "There's something big coming up for ya, Jan. You're gonna make it big." It sounded like a promise. "Some…ah…friends of mine want to meet you." He scribbled an address on a scrap of paper and handed it to me. "They'd like to see you tomorrow at 3. These are powerful people," he said, clenching his fist. "They'll get ya to the top. They wanna work with ya."

"Wonderful! I'll see you there, Bobby?"

"No, no, not me. You just keep the appointment. These men have something really terrific in mind for you. I'll be in touch, OK?"

"OK, Bobby."

I studied the scrap of paper, rereading the scribbled note of the time and place. I was to see a Mr. Luciano.

The next day after the matinee, I ran from the stage door of the theater, flagged a cab, and handed the note with the address to the cabbie. A feeling of uneasiness smothered me.

Traffic in New York is always bad, but that day the streets were completely clogged. The cab had been in motion for some time but seemed to be going nowhere. After several blocks I anxiously asked, "Could you zigzag around these cars, driver?"

"OK, OK," he replied, waving his hand in the air. "I'm trying. What da youse want me ta do?" He wiped his sweaty face and listened to the crackly voice coming through the radio while I fidgeted in the backseat.

It was 2:55, five minutes before what could be the most significant meeting of my career, and I was stuck in city traffic with a jam-up around every corner. The sun was blistering hot and bouncing off the pavement in shimmering waves as we crept along a few more blocks. We were getting close to the address. I ached to tell the driver to stop and let me out, but we weren't in the best part of town. Finally, I said, "Pull over and let me out. I'll get there on foot. A walk will do me good."

"I'm doin' it, lady. Dis here's da place. We're here."

I moved to the edge of the seat to take a better look. "Here?" I had expected an office building of some sort. All I could see was a rundown candy store in a seedy part of Brooklyn.

"Yeah, dis here's it," he said, shoving the scrap of paper at me and pointing to the street number over the storefront.

I peered at grimy shop windows where little children pressed their dirty faces to the glass. "Wait for me," I said, reluctantly stepping from the cab onto the scorching sidewalk. "I don't like the look of this. I have a feeling I'll be right back. It has to be the wrong address." I was surrounded by unsavory-looking characters, screaming kids, and pushcarts.

"Aw, come on, lady!"

"No! Wait for me. Don't leave me here. I'll be right back."

A bell jingled over the door as I hurried inside. The rich aroma of chocolate permeated the dimly lit shop. An electric fan whirred in the corner but did little to cool the steamy air. A heavyset, sullen-looking woman sat behind the counter, her thick black hair pulled behind her head and fastened in a tight bun.

"I'm looking for a Mr. Luciano. I have an appointment."

"In there," she mumbled, pointing to a hall at the back of the shop as she slid off her stool and shuffled across the room.

That's strange, I thought. *She didn't even ask my name.*

"Through here?" I asked.

She nodded. I entered a small hallway where my presence did little to distract a cat batting at a bug in the corner. I looked back toward the lady, who nodded and waved me on. The walls, painted in Kem-Tone green, were in need of a good scrubbing, as was the door at the end of the hall. My heart was racing as I listened to the clicking of my spike heels on the bare wooden floor. My jaws were clenched, but this was more than interview jitters; it was an eerie feeling I couldn't shake. What could a person in this place do for my career? Trying to dismiss any ill thought, I tapped on the door.

A deep muffled voice said, "Come in."

Slowly turning the knob and pulling the door open, I saw a small, sparsely furnished room. A rickety card table and several folding chairs stood in the middle of the floor. On the table a cut-down coffee can was filled with stale cigarette butts that smelled rank, and near the table stood an overflowing wastebasket and a Coke bottle dripping its sticky contents onto the worn linoleum.

Walking to the center of the room, I spotted a distinguished-looking gentleman in a dark-blue suit standing in an adjoining hallway. Apparently I wasn't the only one overdressed for such shabby surroundings.

I spoke hesitantly. "I'm Jan Welles. I have an appointment with Mr. Luciano."

"Yes," the man said. "Please give us a minute. We'll be right with you, Miss Welles."

"But I have a cab waiting," I said, as I moved my foot tentatively toward the exit. I wanted to leave, forget the whole damned offer or whatever it was, and get out of there. My mind was racing. *Bobby must be out of his head,* I thought. *Why on earth would he send me here?*

Walking past me toward the outer hall, the gentleman reached into his pocket and called to the woman in the candy store. "Maria," his deep, demanding voice filled the hallway, "take care of Miss Welles's cab." He flashed a thick fold of money held tightly in a gold money clip and presented her with a $20 bill as she materialized. Turning to me, he said politely, "Give us a moment, please?"

As he turned and opened a door into still another room, I caught a glimpse of brilliant red carpeting and a long conference table where several men were seated. Smoke from their cigars hovered overhead and sent a robust aroma of Havana tobacco wafting into the room. A few moments later another handsomely dressed gentleman, tall and with graying hair, came through the doorway. He approached and introduced himself. "My name is Luciano. I represent a group of investors." Shaking my hand, he invited me into the meeting room. *Keep your back straight,* I directed myself, stretching as tall as my 5-foot-7 frame would allow. Once inside, I looked hard at the six men standing before me, men who might well be determining my future, and I knew at once they weren't ordinary businessmen.

"Gentlemen," I said. "You wanted to see me?"

Mr. Torasio, a stern-looking man with deep lines in his face, greeted me, then dutifully made the introductions. I had the feeling I'd seen a few of them before but thought no more of it. They all appeared to have stepped from a display window at Brooks Brothers. Their hair, dark, some graying, looked as though it had been professionally combed, and their faces were clean-shaven. As they each shook my hand, I noticed their highly buffed, manicured nails and gold jewelry. With each introduction, I pulled in my gut to hide my fear and mounting suspicions.

"We have a contract that will interest you," Mr. Torasio said, as he slid the crisp sheets of paper toward me. Steadying my hand on the shiny rosewood table, I picked up the top sheet.

Mr. Giodonna, a medium-built man with bad skin, began to speak. "We caught your act the other night and think it's brilliant. Like the publicity says, your voice is captivating."

"Thank you very much. I've worked hard."

"It shows, Jan," Mr. Giodonna said. "Now, tell me, how old are you?"

"Thirty-two."

He smiled and nodded. I began reading the contract. There it was—all I had worked for during the past 16 years. I heard my heart pounding and wondered if they could hear it too. *Take a deep breath,* I reminded myself. I tried to look calm, but it was difficult. This was it: Las Vegas and $25,000 a week, the biggest salary I had ever been offered by far. I felt a tightness in my throat as I fought for control.

A quiet tension hung in the air as I read the terms of the offer. Mr. Luciano broke the silence. "Of course, we'll have to have a piece of the action."

"Of course," I said, trying to control my excitement. This was a standard contract. The usual management fees ran between 20 and 40%, and this one was 35%, which was OK.

"Jan," Mr. Luciano continued, "I've taken the liberty of drawing up a second contract. Would you take a look at this also?"

I knew the papers for the second agreement would be a personal contract, but I felt an edginess in his tone regarding the possible additional terms. The other men sat quietly, a table of clones. Only the faint rustle of their suits and the click of gold cuff links on the table broke the silence.

Taking the second contract, I looked into his eyes: They were steel-gray, cold, and penetrating. His face was expressionless, except for a slippery, calculating half-smile and eyes that seemed to cover every part of me. I was amused, and a voice inside wanted to say, "Forget it! This is a disguise!" But I dismissed the thought quickly. After working so long, I could let nothing interfere with this opportunity. My concentration was steady, focusing on each stipulation, when I heard, "And, ah, Miss Welles…"

I looked up from the contract toward Mr. Giodonna. "If there's any item in that agreement that may need explaining, we will be more than happy to clarify it."

"There are a few things," I said. "The contract is for five years, correct?"

"That's right, and after that we can continue the contract indefinitely." Smiling, he added, "Our option can be renewed every five years."

"I understand."

"Take your time, Jan," Mr. Luciano interrupted, "there are several pages."

While I read the contract, the silence of the room seemed to magnify the sound of their breathing and the rattle of the paper as I turned each page. The tension was interrupted by a knock at the door.

Maria, the woman from the candy store, entered the room behind an elegant brass tea cart laden with cut-glass decanters, glasses, and cups, and a large silver container of ice. From the bottom shelf of the cart, she took a finely carved wooden chest of cigars and placed it on the table, then dispensed coffee and bourbon.

I read the last page; the contract covered everything:

benefits, hotel accommodations, foreign travel, all of which carried special stipulations.

Smoky translucent clouds of sweet-smelling tobacco permeated the air and hovered around the faces of the silent men. As the wafts of smoke cleared, I studied their features. Suddenly I remembered. The night before Bobby had disappeared, Giodonna and Torasio had been sitting at a table in the club watching us. Disregarding the significance of my discovery, I continued reading.

The clause pertaining to transportation stated, "Management will select and provide," and I thought of the frightening ride the manager of the Enright Theater had arranged for me when I was a teenager.

I brought up the matter with Mr. Giodonna, who said it was for my own protection. "Sir," I said, "I wonder how I'm protected when traveling in a private car with an escort of your choice?"

"We will be your protection," he laughed. Then, leaning back against the chair, he bragged, "What other protection would you need?"

Studying the clause pertaining to hotel accommodations and other living quarters, I recalled my stay at the Astor Hotel, in a suite offered by my producer.

The flash from a gold cigarette lighter brought me back to reality as Mr. Torasio lit a cigar. Then, in disbelief, I read the provision regarding living arrangements: Again, "Management will select and provide." I raised my head slowly. "Does this mean I'd have nothing to say about where I sleep?" I looked at the faces of the men in the room and waited for an answer.

Mr. Torasio puffed for a moment, then allowed a large ring of smoke to roll from his rounded mouth. "Miss Welles," he said, and his face wore the same arrogant smile as that of Sonny Barbolis when he had removed his clothes in that Acapulco hotel room, "if we're going to build you, we must have control."

"Yes, Mr. Torasio, I agree, but I have to be able to control some parts of my personal life."

He placed his cigar in the ashtray and opened his mouth to speak, but I continued, "If you control my personal life, I won't be the performer you want. Gentlemen, please, give me room! Don't inhibit me. I have to be the person I am."

I stared hard at their faces but got no response. My brain fashioned gargoyle images of the figures around the table as their eyes ogled every part of me except the part that was talking. My feelings of discomfort increased.

"Mr. Luciano, let me be blunt," I said. "What would happen, for instance, if you wanted me to exchange, let's say, favors with someone just for a part in a show or movie?"

There was no response, other than a slight clearing of the throat. Looking around the room to gain perspective, I tried to grasp what was happening. The rich walnut paneling that covered the walls, these expensively dressed men, and the $25,000 a week contract—all in the back of the shabby candy store. Where was this leading and what could I do about it?

"Miss Welles," said one man in a pin-striped suit, "I think you're missing the point." He paused. "This contract," he said, tapping it with his finger, "stands as written. The terms are not negotiable."

For a moment I sat stunned, then I spoke up. "What would happen if I refused to go along with one of your decisions about my career?"

"Miss Welles, that would be a breach of contract, and you would find it difficult to get work anywhere."

"In other words, I'd be blackballed."

"That's correct."

I was in the midst of the Mafia. All I'd have to do was sign the contract, have them find out I was a lesbian, then crawl through the rest of my life—or have nothing. And they could even threaten the lives of my family to make me submit.

Thoughts of past entrapments flashed in my mind: *If I were a man, we could close this deal. As a woman, I haven't got a chance, and for me, life wouldn't be worth living if I signed. I'd be forever fighting to protect myself.*

"Look at the other side," Mr. Torasio piped in. "You're a gorgeous woman. We want to tie in 'Godfrey's Stardust Girl' as featured entertainer with the Stardust Casino. We'll escalate your career. We'll take you to the very top!"

The contract and the looks on their faces had reduced me to an object. I had always been truthful when men approached me, but I could never tell these men the truth. There they sat in their silk shirts and tailor-made suits, offering me an opportunity to let them control my private life. How lucky could I get?

Looking into Mr. Luciano's steel-gray eyes, I recalled my grandmother saying, "You can do anything. You're free!" Signing this would change that. "Gentlemen," I said, sliding the papers across the highly polished table, "I've lived too long and worked too hard to throw away pride for fame." Rising from my chair, I added, "It's not worth it!"

"I hope you'll reconsider our offer," Mr. Luciano said.

"If you change the contract to protect my personal life, we have a deal. But as this is written, no! I won't be your toy to be picked up and delivered to the bed of whatever joker pays you for a good time. I won't be told what to wear, what to take off, or when to lie down. I'm sure you have plenty of women to pick from, but not this one. I've got to be able to wake up in the morning and like the person I see in the mirror, and there's no money, fame, or compensation that could make up for that. So if you people decide you want an artist instead of a good time, let me know. I'm sure you'll know where to find me."

* * *

Outside, the glare and heat of the street engulfed me as I tried to flag a cab. More than anything else, I wanted to take away the afternoon, have it disappear, forget the whole episode as though it hadn't happened.

But I left with my pride and dignity intact, and went back to the theater more determined than ever. *There are a lot of theaters and clubs to work,* I thought. *I've been doing it for 16 years. Morry can get my salary up without them. Of course, it may not be Las Vegas...*

As my engagement at the Palace drew to a close, I received another surprise visit from Bobby in my dressing room.

"How did the appointment go, Jan?"

"Oh, Bobby, don't ask."

"What happened?"

"They want complete control of everything! I couldn't sign the contract. They expect too much."

"What do you mean, you couldn't sign it?" Bobby looked incredulous. "You don't understand, Jan. They want to tie in Godfrey's Stardust Girl with the Stardust Casino as a perma—"

"I know, I know, Bobby."

"Hey, 25 grand a week is big money, Jan, and they want a piece of the action."

"I know!" I nearly screamed.

"They've had their eye on you for a long time."

"Listen, Bobby, I don't have to be a 'star.' I'm doing fine as I am."

Bobby pulled up a chair and sat looking at the floor, as though he were totally defeated. "They got to me, Jan," he said. "All those years ago, they made me leave you alone. They beat me down. Now, everybody has to leave you alone, including Morry. They're fixing it so you'll need them. You gotta sign, Jan, or else..."

"Or else what?" I asked. "What do you mean, 'or else'?"

"Or else they'll fix it so you have a hard time finding work anywhere," Bobby said sadly. "They'll fix it so everybody'll be afraid to manage you."

"So I'll manage myself. I've done it for years! And if I can't work in this country., I'll work in Mexico or Europe. They won't keep me from working! But let's assume I do sign…what happens the first time I say no to one of those bastards trying to get me into bed? I wouldn't just be kicked out of a show, would I, Bobby?"

Bobby continued to stare at the floor.

"No, they'd find a way to force me. Once they learn the truth about my life, do you think they'll be understanding?" I laughed. "Do you really believe they'll respect me and my personal life? Hardly. The world has never been that kind to gay people or any other minority group. Look what they did to the Jews, your people, Bobby. And black folks, as great as Billie Holiday and the Mills Brothers are, they're still barred from some places. It's hard to believe that such a large group of people, who call themselves 'the majority,' can be so damn small!"

"Look, Jan," Bobby started, "I know it's tough, but that's the way it is on the way up. I told you there'd be a time like this. When you'd have to change and…"

"You mean, to reach the pinnacle of my own being, I've got to look like them, think like them, and love like them? They've got their fucking nerve!"

"Well, look, Jan—"

"No! You look, Bobby. I may not be the majority, but don't kid yourself, there are countless millions like me everywhere. We're good people, talented people, we're sitting beside you, and working with you! And, yes, we're even married to you. You know, Bobby, many fine people helped me along the way. I didn't ask what they did in bed—they were good people! And I didn't ask the ones who hurt me. Their deeds told me all I needed to know!"

Bobby sat there, speechless, as I continued, angrier with each passing moment.

"They kept asking for femininity and glamour," I said, "and I gave, not to hide what I am but to please them. Now I've given everything except my private life, and I will give no more. Success or failure…it's going to be my way, because I've got to be true to myself. So if I have to give up working in the States for the right to my own life, I will."

I have no recollection of Bobby leaving. But at least now all the pieces in the puzzle fit.

While preparing for my last show at the Palace, I dressed in the bullfight suit from the waist down, slipped into the ice-blue net gown, and checked the mirror for last-minute details. Then the overture began.

Onstage the hot lights danced in tiny reflections from the sequin swirls on my gown, so feminine, such a farce. I sang one beautiful ballad after the other, and the applause was deafening. Then came the blackout. Offstage I listened to the ovation as the dresser unzipped my gown and let it fall in a circle around me. I looked at the gown on the floor and at the rhinestone bracelets and earrings that were such a disguise, and as I stepped over the mound of net that circled my feet I felt alive.

I realized that I had been underneath all those frills, hiding, leading myself into an unnatural existence, giving them something to want—something that was ultimately unattainable.

The audience's response continued as the dresser held a mirror in front of me for a final check. "Here you are," I whispered, "begging for acceptance and giving them a masquerade."

While I adjusted my jacket, cummerbund, and tie, I heard the master of ceremonies begin the introduction to the bullfight sequence. During the performance, my mind flashed vivid pictures of what the audience had been seeing when they watched me onstage. I recalled the "tags" all the critics had given me: "Cinderella," "sexy chanteuse," "flame-haired honey." How could society accept me when I'd been offering them a different persona?

The orchestra began the introduction to my closing number, "I'm Gonna Live Till I Die." In my head the music was a blur of sound, punctuated by Bobby's words: "Ya still got 'em fooled, haven't ya, girl!" *And as long as they're fooled, I'll have to keep fighting*, I thought. So what difference does it make what kind of arena you're in, if you're next to a bull with your face in the sand or with six men at a rosewood table? If you don't like the smell, you get out.

On cue I sang with every fiber of my being. I gave to them in unqualified dimensions as I sang to the highest balcony, to the last row, with my last song. As I held that final note, the applause began and continued as the pinspot widened and the entire stage became a flood of light.

Single roses were thrown onto the stage, and people in the lower balconies stretched their arms as I moved closer to them. With the spotlight following me to the side of the stage, I turned to those wonderful people and solemnly vowed to myself, *For as long I live, so help me God, I will never hide again.*

$\mathcal{E}$pilogue

One week after closing at the Palace, I was hired as a manager with a major company on Fifth Avenue in New York; I retired in 1982. For the past 23 years I've been living with the love of my life, Diana, in the home we had always dreamed of, with floor-to-ceiling glass, low white sofas, and gold brocade pillows.

In January 1993, as the masses fixed their attention on President Clinton's attempt to allow homosexuals to serve their country, I thought of the relentless hours I had spent entertaining servicemen and women at hospitals and at Army, Navy, Marine, and Air Force bases throughout the country. I thought of the gay people in uniform I had met who had given their lives so that *all* U.S. citizens could remain free. We lesbians and gay men are here. We are living and working beside you. You may not recognize most of us because we're not marching. We're not demonstrating.

But we're not hiding. We are here. We are the silent voices.